1 OF 1 MUSCLE CARS

Stories of Detroit's Rarest Iron

CarTech®

WES EISENSCHENK

CarTech®

CarTech®, Inc.
6118 Main Street
North Branch, MN 55056
Phone: 651-277-1200 or 800-551-4754
Fax: 651-277-1203
www.cartechbooks.com

CarTech books may be purchased at a discounted rate in bulk for resale, events, corporate gifts, or educational purposes. Special editions may also be created to specification. For details, contact Special Sales at 6118 Main Street, North Branch, MN 55056 or by email at sales@cartechbooks.com.

Edit by Bob Wilson
Layout by Connie DeFlorin

ISBN 978-1-61325-800-2
Item No. CT697

Library of Congress Cataloging-in-Publication Data Available

Written, edited, and designed in the U.S.A.
Printed in China
10 9 8 7 6 5 4 3 2 1

All photos are courtesy of Wes Eisenschenk unless otherwise noted.

Front Flap: Dick Harrell drives an LS6-equipped 454 1970 Nova. Harrell prepped and sold a handful of these cars, but their current whereabouts are not known.

DISTRIBUTION BY:

Europe
PGUK
63 Hatton Garden
London EC1N 8LE, England
Phone: 020 7061 1980 • Fax: 020 7242 3725
www.pguk.co.uk

Australia
Renniks Publications Ltd.
3/37-39 Green Street
Banksmeadow, NSW 2109, Australia
Phone: 2 9695 7055 • Fax: 2 9695 7355
www.renniks.com

Canada
Login Canada
300 Saulteaux Crescent
Winnipeg, MB, R3J 3T2 Canada
Phone: 800 665 1148 • Fax: 800 665 0103
www.lb.ca

Publisher's Note: In reporting history, the images required to tell the tale will vary greatly in quality, especially by modern photographic standards. While some images in this volume are not up to those digital standards, we have included them, as we feel they are an important element in telling the story.

Table of Contents

ACKNOWLEDGMENTS

I thought that I was done after writing *Lost Muscle Cars* and *1969 Plymouth Road Runner: Muscle Cars in Detail No. 5*. However, like a gambler who must put one more quarter into the slot machine, I decided to come out of "retirement" to offer you these compelling tales. As with *Lost Muscle Cars*, I hope some of these stories will help you discover some of these machines.

Hopefully, your family has supported your hobby and career much like mine has. Thanks as always to my lovely wife, Michelle. Without her, I wouldn't have had the opportunity to own some of the rarest muscle cars in the world. Her support and dedication to research whenever I purchase something odd and unusual drives me to keep finding more of the odd and unusual.

Elliott, Bailee, and Maize are the fuel that keeps me centered in this hobby. I've lost count of the times I've looked in the rearview mirror after lifting off the gas in a tire-burning pull through the gears. Their grins and smiles from the back seat tell me all that I need to know about the apple not falling far from the tree.

Thanks to Mom and Dad for their continued presence in this hobby that I so enjoy. After this book hits the shelves, we are bringing Mom's 1973 Javelin to the Muscle Car and Corvette Nationals (MCACN). What did I say about the apple not falling far from the tree?

This book would not be complete without the wonderful support from fellow hobbyists and bonified experts in their respective fields: Thomas Benvie, Charlie Henry, Trev Dellinger, Scott Kolecki, Todd Zuercher, Alan Munro, Mark Sekula, Matti Färm, DK Nakadashi, Bill Adams, Rick Nelson, Billy and Jennifer Pope, Mark Pieloch/Ed Dedick, Brian Styles, Tom Clary, Duncan Brown, and Colin Comer.

If you have a compelling 1 of 1 car to share, don't hesitate to reach out and let me know what you have.

Scan this QR code to visit the "Lost Muscle Cars" Facebook page.

INTRODUCTION

"1 of 1." In some circles, that phrase is a cringe-worthy expression. Many times, it's used to attribute exclusivity and rarity to a vehicle.

"Hey man, I have a 1969 Mach 1 with a 351 and a 3-speed manual. It's Champagne Gold with power front discs, the AM radio, and the Visibility Group. It's the only one that was built like that on May 25, 1969. This is *that* car!"

Every car ever built can be drilled down to 1 of 1. Why write a book about such a mundane muscle-car phrase? The reason is because there were some seriously bad-ass cars created that wear this phrase well.

Creating a formula that maintains a level of rarity and excitement while not drilling down to trivial details, such as hood-pad insulation and passenger-side remote mirrors, as criteria is open for debate. How far down is too far down?

Clearly, some of a car's core components should be considered. The engine, transmission, and color seem to be agreed upon by most who've attempted the impossible task of defining the significant criteria for a 1 of 1 consideration. Noteworthy options might be considered as well. If a production model, such as the 1969 Boss 429, had a singular list of options available, yet somehow one snuck out with air

You will be reading more about the **Lawman** *in a few pages. The whereabouts of Al Eckstrand's Sweden-delivered 1970 Mach 1s are unknown. Just like the heralded Vietnam-delivered cars that were for the soldiers to test drive, several Mustangs were sent to Sweden in the fall of 1969 for tour duty. (Photo Courtesy Per Olaf)*

conditioning, shouldn't that be considered 1 of 1? How about a 1970 'Cuda 340 convertible? It might not sound rare, but what if it's the only one ever built with a shaker hood?

Luckily, there's no need to stew on what makes a car 1 of 1. I'll do that for you.

All the cars featured in the following pages have a compelling story and fall into three sections: 1) prototypes and special factory builds, 2) factory production cars, and 3) super-car tuners and builders.

Prototypes and special factory builds are all tied to a manufacturer that looked to design and develop a car for mass production. Some of these cars became engineering mules. Others were built to placate a cozy relationship with a higher-up within the corporate walls. Some were built to test something that may have ended up on the cutting-room floor.

The category of factory production cars is the most scrutinized. For my inclusion as a 1 of 1, the mass-production muscle car must have a unique engine, transmission, or color; and the vehicle it was created for must have been made available to the general public. Anyone could have walked into a dealership and ordered this car. Maybe you had to *know* someone to buy it.

I also take into consideration items such as the rear-end gear ratio and the aforementioned items, such as a shaker hood or air conditioning. I'll await your book if you want to arm wrestle over my criteria.

White Bear Dodge built this blown Plum Crazy 1970 Dodge Challenger with a 426 Hemi. By all accounts, it was to test the market to possibly compete against Mr. Norm in the dealer-built super-car world. A prospective buyer noted that it was listed for $8,000 in 1970. (Photo Courtesy Jim Perkl)

Lastly, we have the super-car tuners. These third-party builders took a production muscle car and put their own spin on it. The conversion had to take place in the same model year the car was offered. All of these cars are one step removed from manufacturer support. Typically, a dealership or regional manager created a new version of the car and advertised it in a magazine, newspaper, or on the radio. They weren't one-offs, but due to their rarity and survival rate, they are likely the only current representatives of those creations. They may not survive today, but they were recorded as having existed once upon a time.

So, there you have it: 1 of 1.

Having invested 24 hours a day, 7 days a week, and 365 days a year for the last 20 years into dedicated research on rare muscle cars, I feel fortunate to share many cars that you may have never heard of before. Some of these stories were facilitated by respected hobbyists who spent decades honing their craft into understanding these cars. To that, I yield my expertise to them and offer these pages so they can tell you a story.

I'm sure we didn't include some very worthy muscle cars. For that, I apologize. 1 of 1 Part 2, anyone?

CHAPTER 1

Prototypes and Special Factory Builds

Mass-produced muscle cars drive the sector of the hobby that we all enjoy. The millions of Chargers, Chevelles, Mustangs, Javelins, and GTOs that were constructed have pulled along an incredible aftermarket industry that fuels passion for them. The story of all these cars began somewhere.

Some of the cars in this chapter were a response to a competitor that found success in a niche part of the market. Others were a wild hair up someone's ass, and that person had the authority to bring it to fruition. All of them had one thing in common: factory support.

Each car in this chapter likely had the idea run all the way up the flagpole for approval and back down to the respective division for its creation. That creation likely appeared on an existing platform and wasn't a new creation from scratch.

In most cases, these cars were not supposed to leave the manufacturer and be allowed into the hands of the buying public. As we know, sometimes things slip through the cracks.

Cars in this chapter are a bit Ford heavy. The simple reason for this is that Ford allowed cars to slip through the cracks at a much higher rate than its competitors. Ford's legendary resale lot was only available to employees. Some cars were delivered there on purpose, and some employees cut backdoor deals to have a car sent there. Either way, it's the reason for the higher survival rate for Ford prototypes and factory builds.

1968 OLDSMOBILE FOURANADO 4-4-2

By BK Nakadashi

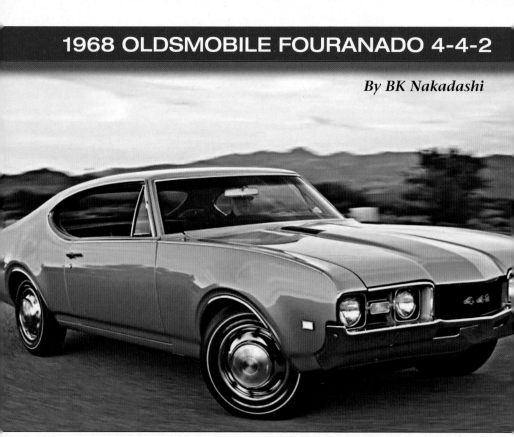

The deceptive look of the 4-4-2 Toronado wants you to believe this is nothing more than a production model. In truth, the car is 2.5 inches longer than a stock 4-4-2, and it's front-wheel drive. (Photo Courtesy Jeff Koch/Hemmings Motor News)

George Hurst is a legendary name in muscle-era performance cars. He frequently did what the factory could not or would not do. The man, whose name is synonymous with rugged, fast-action performance-car shifters for all marques, began building limited-run cars in the latter half of the 1960s. Oldsmobile was a reasonable place to start, considering his national success with the twin-Toronado-powered *Hurst Hairy Oldsmobile* drag car.

In mid-1968, Hurst helped Oldsmobile worm its way around GM's mandated 400-ci maximum displacement in intermediate cars and created the Hurst/Olds, which was an A-Body built by Hurst (technically) with 455 ci beneath the hood. The company built 515 of them in that truncated first year, proving that all of that power and torque made an extraordinary automobile.

Frankenstein's Oldsmobile

With that crowd-pleasing, twin-engine, all-wheel-drive strip monster and the original 455-powered, corporate-edict-beating Hurst/Olds street car, the men who ran Lansing needed a proof-of-concept for the proposed street car. Hurst and his gang of engineers built what proved to be the missing link between the two. They split the difference between the conventional-but-better approach and the wild four-smoking-tire freak-out that was touring the country. Behold the Fouranado: a new-for-1968 Oldsmobile 4-4-2 with the W-34 Toronado driveline, including a chain-driven GMTH425 front-wheel-drive transaxle.

Oldsmobile's muscle car was newly styled for the year with its semi-fastback roofline, Toronado-esque blistered fenders, and more. The sporty body hid a driveline and chassis that were largely carried over. Although, the new chassis was slightly shorter, at 112 inches between the wheel centers. The Toronado, a front-wheel-drive personal-luxury sensation that launched in the fall of 1965, offered

*A 400-hp 455 Rocket V-8 propelled the Toronado. Underneath, the Toronado's frame was mated to the 4-4-2 frame, and the driveshaft hump was flattened. (Photo Courtesy Jeff Koch/*Hemmings Motor News*)*

something new for 1968: 455 ci of power. The standard Toro 455 was rated at 375 hp, but keen enthusiasts ordered the W-34 option, a 400-hp variant of the 455, which was Toronado's first-ever optional engine. The extra 25 hp was freed up thanks to a higher-lift cam and more-freely-flowing dual exhaust. Separately, major elements across two Oldsmobile lines were new for 1968. It was Hurst's genius to combine them.

At first blush, the Fouranado looks stock—like a 4-4-2 with chrome Toronado wheels and Goodyear Blue Streaks. In truth, the Fouranado is far wilder than that. Fitting the driveline came first, and other changes were made to accommodate it. The Fouranado began as an early-production 4-4-2 that was painted black. It had many options, including power windows, a power driver's seat, reclining passenger's seat, power trunk release, AM/FM/8-track player with power antenna, and air conditioning. A W-34 driveline was used as well as some preproduction suspension bits that were rescued from the proving grounds in Michigan.

The Toronado's frame joined the 4-4-2's frame mid-car, and a newly-fabricated flat floor increased room inside. The standard rear axle was replaced with a solid-beam axle and had a standard 4-4-2 coil-spring and trailing-arm suspension. The front wheel openings were pushed 2.5 inches forward compared to the stock A-Body. It was subtly sectioned, and the radiator core support was also altered. The car was painted with the same shade of gold as seen on the *Hurst Hairy Oldsmobile* to create the Fouranado.

Naming the Beast

Super Stock and *Car Craft* magazines both took a crack at naming the result. The Fouranado name came from the *Super Stock* piece. The men who ran Lansing liked what they saw but opted for something more conventional: the 1968 Hurst/Olds that we have known and loved for the past five decades. What happened to the Fouranado? As far as anyone can tell, George Hurst used it as his personal ride for a few years, although details from that time period are unclear.

Into Public Hands

The history of the Fouranado continued in the spring of 1970. The nearest Oldsmobile dealership to Hurst Performance Engineering's

Southern California base was Guy Martin Oldsmobile in Woodland Hills. The Fouranado made the cover of the dealership's monthly magazine. This intrigued William Hesse, who bought it and used it as a daily driver in Southern California through 1973, in New Jersey between 1973 and 1976, and then in Oklahoma City, where William parked it a decade later with 116,000 miles on the odometer. It sat in that Oklahoma garage for more than 25 years.

This is when longtime Oldsmobile A-Body enthusiast Fred Mandrick of Scottsdale, Arizona, entered the picture. When he bought Mark Fletcher and Richard Truesdell's *Hurst Equipped* book, he immediately perused the Oldsmobile stories and then rediscovered the Fouranado. Wes Eisenchenk put Fred and William in contact with each other. It didn't take long for the two to come to an arrangement in late 2012. Fred even got documentation—from warranty paperwork to the original black California plates.

The Fouranado was awakened from its incognito slumber when author and Hurst historian Mark Fletcher discovered the car. Discoveries such as these keep the phrase "they're still out there" in vogue. (Photo Courtesy Richard Truesdell)

Restoration

The new owner weighed the pros and cons of restoration versus preservation, and he decided that the Fouranado was rough enough that he needed to restore it as close as possible to the original. Fred set a goal for himself: show it off at the 2013 Muscle Car and Corvette Nationals (MCACN), which was held the weekend before Thanksgiving in Chicago. That left less than one year to disassemble and reassemble a 1 of 1, four-plus-decade-old, hand-built machine that looked stock but really wasn't.

Disassembly uncovered surprises that were bad (broken piston rings in two of the cylinders) and good (a number stamped into the block that indicated this 455 was a prototype or experimental engine). Care was taken to document and later replicate factory markings, such as a hand-written "XP" on one side of the block, and a green paint splash on the other. The most aggressive changes were that the block was bored 0.030 over, resized rods and Keith Black pistons were installed to replicate the 10.25:1 compression, and the valve seats were hardened. The camshaft had no markings on it and was replaced with a factory-style W-34 cam.

The TH425 revealed a surprise during the rebuild: a 3.54 final-drive ratio, degrees hairier than the 3.07 that came in every other 1966–1970 Toronado. The prototype suspension and engine components were painted blue on the front half-shafts with yellow torsion bars, but Fred elected to refinish them in standard factory hues.

Todd Hood at Hood's Etc. took care of the bodywork and massaged out body dings, sorted a dent in one of the rear quarters, stripped the paint largely by hand (except for the doorjambs, which were done via glass beads in a solution), and cleaned up several unfinished issues from the original conversion, including some underbody bracing and firewall finishing.

The sections in the front fenders were coming apart and allegedly took 80 hours each to sort out. The paint color was derived from areas that had been hidden under trim for 45 years, rather than guessing from a paint chart or book. Inside, the black vinyl interior was largely Lansing-built, except for the flat floor, the Dual Gate shifter, a console that Hurst's shop whipped up, and a golden-flaked NOS shift handle. Fred completed the final assembly himself.

At the 2013 MCACN event, the Fouranado won the Best Display award as well as the Celebrity Choice award from the editor of *Hemmings Muscle Machines* magazine. It was a fitting reward for this missing link of muscle cars.

1969 MERCURY COUGAR BOSS 429

By Wes Eisenschenk

Kar-Kraft employees pose for staged photos inside the Merriman location. Centered in this frame is the 1969 Boss 429 Cougar XR-7 prototype with the distinctive air cleaner snorkel. (Photo Courtesy Fran Hernandez Family Archives)

Just like a good fishing tale, the saga of the 1969 Boss 429 Cougars was told in some fanciful stories over the years. At first, they didn't exist. Then, only two existed. After more research, four confirmed cars were built. What is fact and what is fiction when it comes to Mercury's attempt in procuring and utilizing Ford's newest big-block powerplant for its beloved pony car?

To tell the tale, let's begin with Richard Petty. Yes, *that* Richard Petty. King Richard was a thorn in the side of Ford Motor Company throughout the 1960s. Petty's 27 wins (10 in a row) in 1967 was the ass-kicking that Ford needed to begin the process to try to dethrone the king.

Ford Racing

Ford was used to overcoming the competition. In 1966 and 1967, it won Trans-Am championships in the first two seasons of the series. In 1966, Ford body-slammed Ferrari at Le Mans and beat it into submission by winning four straight races (1966 to 1969). In the dirt, Broncos won four out of five Baja 1000s in the 4-wheel class (1968, 1969, 1971, and 1972). In 1968 at Pomona, Ford's new Cobra Jet Mustang featured an all-Ford final with Al Joniec winning on a red light against Hubert Platt in the coveted SS/E finals. Ford doubled-up at Indy with Jerry Harvey winning the SS/E class at the U.S. Nationals.

With only one championship in NASCAR (1965), Ford wanted to carve a deeper gorge into the competition in stock car racing. It did so in 1968 when David Pearson won the Grand National Championship and edged Bobby Isaac and Richard Petty. Pearson and Petty had 11 wins each. Unlike the other manufacturers that Ford competed against in other series, Mopar wasn't going away quietly into the night. Chrysler liked winning in NASCAR, and 1969 was shaping up to be a fight for the ages.

Aero Wars

The seesaw battle for superspeedway supremacy started when Dodge began looking at ways to make the Charger more aerodynamic.

After getting spanked in the 1968 Daytona 500 by Ford, Chrysler used the 1968 racing season to finesse the aesthetics of its Charger and created the sleek Charger 500. A flush grille, flush rear window, and new A-pillar gave the Charger a competitive advantage and made them slippery on superspeedways. The only problem was that Ford was doing the same thing to its Cyclones and Torinos to gear up for the 1969 racing season.

Not only was Ford matching Chrysler punch for punch in the aerodynamics department, it was secretly creating its own version of the Hemi engine for NASCAR competition.

King Kong 2.0

As the tried-and-true 427 FE engine reached the twilight of its life, Ford actively looked for its replacement. The result was the Boss 429. Developed in the latter half of 1968, the Boss 429 and the sleek new Ford Torinos and Cyclones were poised to finally put Chrysler and Richard Petty out to pasture. However, as fate would have it, Petty was unhappy with Plymouth's development of an aero counterpart to the Charger. The Road Runner that he was campaigning was fine for the short tracks (Petty won 16 races in 1968), but on the sexier big-oval tracks, driving the Plymouth was like trying to fly a box through the wind. In a mouth-gaping move, Petty defected to Ford on November 25, 1968.

1969

For homologation purposes, Semon "Bunkie" Knudsen decided that the Mustang should receive the new Boss 429, as he thought it would be next to impossible to move 500 full-size or midsize overpriced vehicles. NASCAR never demanded that production models were needed to homologate an engine, although body modifications took place on the cars that were running in the series.

Ford was busy cranking out its production Boss 429 Mustangs and ceremoniously announced that Job #1 was completed on January 15, 1969. The completion of the task at hand occurred on March 30, 1969, when Cale Yarborough parked his Cyclone in victory lane at Atlanta Motor Speedway.

What about Us!?

While the designers and marketers in the Torino, Mustang, and Cyclone divisions toasted to their own success, the brass in the Cougar division counted the ways that they were screwed over in this deal.

In a December 13, 1968, memo from M.S. McLaughlin (Ford's vice president and division general manager) to R.R. Cosner, McLaughlin noted the following:

"As you know, we have requested that the Special Vehicles activity supply Cougar cars equipped with the street version of the 429 NASCAR engine at the earliest possible date.

"On a basis paralleling the announced Ford Division program, Mr. Passino has agreed to furnish this Division [with] one 429 Cougar by the end of December for promotional purposes, provided an engine is made available by Engine and Foundry Division.

"The purpose of this letter is to request [that] this engine be shipped to the Special Vehicles Brighton plant for this purpose. We would greatly appreciate your expedited handling of this request."

The Prototype Boss 429 Cougar

The Cougar referenced in the note by McLaughlin likely referred to the Boss 429 Cougar prototype. This car carried the brass tag number 178-D-392 and was three digits away from Boss 429 prototype KK1201. This car was ordered on November 15, 1968, and was ripe with options.

The XR-7 featured Burnt Orange paint with a white vinyl top, a white leather bucket-seat interior, Ram Air induction, power windows, the sports console, power steering, power front disc brakes, a tilt-away steering wheel, hood pins, comfort stream ventilation, and an AM radio. The drivetrain consisted of the 428 Cobra Jet engine with a 4-speed Toploader transmission and high-performance 3.50 Traction-Lok rear axle.

The build order noted that the car was a "Special Purpose Vehicle" and was for internal use based on its district sales office (DSO) and dealer number designations. The car was built and sold on December 6, 1968.

The next discussion regarding the prototype came in a memo on March 14, 1969. McLaughlin sent a memo to H.C. MacDonald responding to a March 3 letter regarding the availability of the 429 NASCAR engines for 1969. The letter stated, "We will proceed with the approved program to build fifty (50) Cougars with 429 NASCAR engines to permit homologation for NHRA drag racing, with a time target [of] Springnationals."

McLaughlin requested that the 429 NASCAR engines be released for four Cougars: one for the Special Vehicles prototype, one for the magazine car, and a car each for two drag racers.

Drag Boss 429s

As the ball moved forward internally with plans to produce the homologation prerequisite of 50 units, Ford got a head start on the program by outfitting "Dyno" Don Nicholson and "Fast" Eddie Schartman with Boss 429 Cougars. A pair of consecutive-vehicle identification number (VIN) base-model Cougar two-door hardtops were selected. Both cars were Wimbledon White with a 4-speed

Product Development Group
Ford Motor Company

Rotunda Drive at Southfield
Dearborn, Michigan 48121

April 30, 1969

Mr. Donald Nicholson
604 Vista Del Playa
Orange, California

Dear Mr. Nicholson:

The purpose of this letter is to set forth our understanding with respect to your purchase from the Ford Motor Company of a 1969 429 CID Cougar automobile to be used by you in "drag strip" racing events.

We shall sell to you and you shall buy from us, for One Dollar ($1) and other valuable consideration, one 1969 429 Cougar automobile Serial Number 9F91R567773 . Upon your submission to us of a receipt evidencing the amount paid by you, we shall reimburse you the full amount of any state sales tax that you are obligated to pay in conjunction with your purchase of this vehicle. You shall use the vehicle so purchased by you hereunder to compete in "drag strip" races. You shall use the said 1969 429 Cougar vehicle exclusively in any "drag strip" races in which you compete during the term of this Agreement. You shall retain title to the vehicle sold hereunder during the term of this Agreement. Should you fail to perform, for any reason whatsoever, any of the terms and conditions of this Agreement, you will return this vehicle, upon Ford's written request, to Ford Motor Company without further payment or remuneration to yourself.

It is further understood and agreed between us that said 1969 Cougar automobile will be used for "drag strip" racing only, and shall not be used as a passenger car on public highways. Accordingly, we make no warranty whatsoever, either express or implied, including any warranty of fitness or merchantability, in connection with the sale of this vehicle to you.

It is further understood and agreed that you authorized Ford Motor Company, its advertising agencies and nominees, to use, display, print and publish your name and/or likeness in connection with your use of the vehicle hereinbefore mentioned without further consideration or remuneration to you.

Truck in falle

...memo to Don Nicolson on April 30, 1969, denotes that he will be able to purchase ...Boss 429 Cougar for the sum of $1. Later, these factory-backed drag cars were ...erred to as "dollar cars." (Photo Courtesy Ed Meyer)

transmission and Drag Pak rear end. The "Cougar NASCAR Package" was selected for both cars as an option, and they carried brass tag numbers 178-D-469 (Nicholson) and 178-D-470 (Schartman). Nicholson's car became KK1684, and Schartman's car was tagged KK1685. These KK numbers fall between Mustang Boss 429 production cars. Both cars also had R-code VINs that were retained after conversion. Mustangs arrived at Kar-Kraft with R-code VINs but were converted to Z-code cars upon completion.

The orders were received on April 15, 1969. Kar-Kraft engineer Don Eichstaedt spent the better part of two days babysitting the two Cougars as they traversed the Brighton Kar-Kraft assembly plant on April 23 and 24, 1969. The cars carried a manufactured retail price of $3,936.20 but were "leased" to the racers for a single dollar.

A letter to Don Nicholson on April 30, 1969, outlined the terms of the agreement in which he would campaign the 1969 429 Cougar in drag-strip racing events. Nicholson was not to use the car as a passenger vehicle on public highways. Ford was free to use his likeness in its print and advertising campaigns. Nicholson would "retain [the] title to the vehicle sold hereunder during the term of this agreement."

Both cars underperformed at the track. It wasn't long before Nicholson pulled the Boss 429 and replaced it with his tried-and-true 427 Cammer engine. However, it was to no avail. Schartman campaigned his for a while longer, updated it to a 1970 Cougar, and used it for his Hi Performance Clinics.

"Fast Eddie" Schartman launches his 1969 Boss 429 Cougar against the Jenkins & Retting Bros. race Hemi 1968 Dart.

Magazine Car?

Perhaps the most interesting part in the March 14 letter is the mention of an existing "magazine car." The letter also provided the following information as a bullet point:

"Converting the existing magazine car from a 429 prototype to a 429 Holman-Moody engine and appropriate trim and paint changes. To be handled by Kar Kraft or Nicholson/Yunick and funded as part of the magazine car budget. (Cougar Eliminator Program blue letter dated February 17, 1969.)"

Could the prototype created on November 15, 1968, be the magazine car? A May 1969 company vehicle register for Kar-Kraft lists brass tag 178-D-392 as a "Boss 429 Prototype." Visually, its options mirror the car at the Kar-Kraft Merriman location, and a Boss 429 air cleaner is clearly shown on the car. It could be that the magazine car and the existing prototype were one and the same, and the program was killed prior to the creation of the Special Vehicles prototype.

What we *do* know is that just this one street variant of the Boss 429 Cougar in XR-7 trim has been discovered so far. Could it have survived the crusher at Ford? Absolutely.

Conversations with former Kar-Kraft staffers and experts in the hobby noted rumors of this car having been shipped to the United Kingdom (UK) and to John Woolfe Racing. However, conversations with the alleged recipient of the B9 Cougar determined that John Woolfe Racing wasn't the fortunate beneficiary. Additional research, including a VIN search, in the UK also failed to yield results.

The next time you see a Burnt Orange 1969 XR-7 with white guts and a white hat, check that VIN for an "R." You may have found the long-lost 1969 Boss 429 Cougar prototype.

1969 DODGE DART SWINGING BEE AND DODGE MERADA CHARGER

By Wes Eisenschenk

The Hurst-built Dart Swinging Bee and the Charger Merada pose on a desolate road. Hurst always looked for an opportunity to create a car that a manufacturer would green light and allow them to be built en masse. (Photo Courtesy Bob Lichty Collection)

George Hurst had long been involved in the automotive aftermarket industry and was famously known for his shifters. Hurst had carved a niche by creating custom bumper guards on Volkswagens and aftermarket engine mounts for customers who swapped bigger engines into cars. By 1963, he boasted 100 employees, and his customers included Buick, Chrysler, Dodge, Plymouth, and Pontiac.

With the success of the 1968 Hurst/Olds and the Hemi and 440 Dart and Barracuda programs, the Hurst Performance team of Dave Landrith and Bob Tarrozi called on R.B. McCurry, then head of the Dodge Division, to look for another car program partner for 1970. Hurst purchased two production cars and created a prototype of each model to present to the Chrysler marketing team in March 1969.

Swinging Bee

The first proposal was a bright yellow and black bumblebee-striped 383-powered Dart GTS two-door hardtop with a few Hurst items borrowed from the 1969 Hurst production runs. The vacuum-operated

Ram Air flapper built into the hood utilized a Ford door and actuator, as did the SC/Rambler. The Hurst emblems were the "H" from an H/O with the addition of a bumblebee cartoon character that had a V-8 and headers on its back and wore a racing helmet and goggles. The

The Dart Swinging Bee had a "business in the front, party in the back" appearance. Fresh air was fed through the air scoop while the bee striping flanked the rear quarters of the not-so-subtle Dart.

The Hurst Swinging Bee featured the brand's badge along with a nod to the Scat Pack bee for a logo. (Photos Courtesy Bob Lichty Collection)

name "Swinging Bee" was in bold black letters above the caricature.

The Dart was available with either a Hurst 4-speed shifter or an optional Hurst Dual Gate shifter in the factory console. The top of the console received a bright-colored cover to match the Sunrise Yellow exterior. The exterior of the Bee had a subtle fiberglass hood scoop molded onto the factory steel hood and a small spoiler along the back edge of the trunk. Both proposals had a black interior and sported bullet-style, body-color mirrors as found on the SC/Rambler and Hurst/Olds.

The Charger's gaping Air Grabber hood was set farther back than it was on what became the production-model 1970 GTX and Road Runners. The mesh grille below was called the "shark mouth."

The faux side scoops were reminiscent of the Coronet R/T model that was offered the same year. The Merada had two distinct side colors that traversed from the faux scoops: orange on top and red on the bottom. (Photo Courtesy Bob Lichty Collection)

Merada

Hurst presented the Dodge Merada Charger to compete with the Hurst Pontiac Grand Prix SSJ (and most likely the H/O) as a new category of executive performance cars created over the previous two years. It was equipped as a Charger RT with the 440 V-8 engine, heavy-duty suspension, and a 4-speed manual or 3-speed automatic transmission. It was finished in a dark Sunset Orange with pewter side accents.

This car had two unique design components that quickly identified it as different from a stock Charger. One was the enlarged lower grille opening, which created an open-mouth effect below the front bumper. The second was a hood scoop that was flush with the hood while closed, but it opened up like a clamshell under full acceleration and the subsequent lower engine vacuum.

Although Hurst promoted its prowess by creating exciting cars, it may have inadvertently been feeding product ideas to the Dodge boys. Neither Hurst proposal was accepted by Dodge, but both may have influenced the marketing of special Dodge models that spanned the next two years.

The 1970 model year saw the introduction of the Dart Swinger with a wide bumblebee stripe and dual-scoop Ram Air hood. The 1970 Road Runner and 1971 Charger featured an Air Grabber hood scoop that was flush when closed and opened like a clamshell under acceleration. Both prototypes were very similar to the Hurst Merada design, and both were sold by Hurst to private parties around 1971. Their current whereabouts are unknown.

The Knudsen Boss 429 shows off its distinctive gold hues in Larry Thomas's driveway. (Photo Courtesy Larry Thomas)

We've all read or heard about the famous "aero wars" in NASCAR during the late 1960s. Dodge and Plymouth were in an automotive dispute with Ford and Mercury about who could build the fastest and most slippery car for superspeedway supremacy. Ultimately, there was no true winner, as Ford officially pulled out of sanctioned motorsports on December 5, 1970. But that doesn't mean there aren't a few great untold stories from NASCAR's greatest era.

The Mopar-versus-Ford punch and counterpunch hit its zenith in 1969. NASCAR instituted mandates on production cars to homologate usage of these vehicles for racing. Specifically, if Ford wanted to debut a new motor, it needed that motor to be installed in 500 production cars. Ford had been working on the development of a new 429, semi-hemi motor, and its destination was between the fenders of the Galaxie. By mid-1969, the program was in development, as a handful of Boss 429 Galaxies were created for prototype work. Ford president Semon "Bunkie" Knudsen, sensed the difficult task of convincing 500 buyers to plunk down a small fortune on a rocket-ship ocean liner. He decided that to get the greatest bang for his buck, he needed to ram this elephant between the fenders of Ford's flagship car: the Mustang.

Kar-Kraft

There was one problem with Bunkie's plan. There was no way the Boss 429 would fit between the shock towers of the Mustang. With that, Ford utilized its third-party contractor Kar-Kraft, Inc. to make this dream into a reality.

Ford had utilized Kar-Kraft since the mid-1960s. Kar-Kraft had one client, Ford, and had assisted in the creation of cars, including the Ford GT40 and Trans-Am Mustangs, as well as prototype work on various projects, including the Mach 2A and Can AM G7A race car. Kar-Kraft had multiple locations that were utilized for other Ford projects, such as building Bunkie's personal cars (more on that later) and skunkworks Ford projects. Kar-Kraft was up to the task to create the Boss 429 Mustang.

From the front, the Mercury Cougar scoop that adorns the hood is visible. Bunkie's car was KK1205, which was one of the first seven prototypes built at Kar-Kraft, and it retained an R-code status. Later production Boss 429s had a "Z" in the VIN. This scoop was applied by Kar-Kraft before the Boss 429 scoop was available. (Photo Courtesy Larry Thomas)

Seven Ford Mustangs were earmarked for prototype work and carried the load to develop the street cars for Ford's homologation process. KK1201 was used to qualify brake work and the redistribution of weight. KK1202 was used as a design aid for other affected areas. KK1203 was put through its paces on Ford's rough roads and hammered into a wall at 30 mph for crash testing. KK1204 was the general durability car and had a 406 between it fenders. KK1205 was Bunkie Knudsen's personal car. KK1206 was used for drag testing and ultimately given to Mickey Thompson. KK1207 was the engine-fitment vehicle.

The last vehicle, which didn't receive a KK number, was used for aesthetics development. In all, these eight cars began the process to bring the Boss 429 (B9) to fruition.

One of these B9s was designated for company president Bunkie Knudsen. Yes, it was good to be the man in charge.

KK1205 was one of the prototype Boss 429s created by Kar-Kraft for Ford Motor Company, but more importantly, it was built for one purpose: to appease the boss. Aesthetically, Bunkie's car was quite different than the cars that followed on the production line. Bunkie's car had a striking resemblance to that of Trans-Am and NASCAR owner/builder Smokey Yunikc's Boss 302. The car wore black paint with a gold 1969 Boss 302 stripe with a "429" in its place, and a gold hood, decklid, and tail panel. Inside, Bunkie's B9 featured a rolled and pleated saddle interior with a 4-speed transmission and air conditioning. There were 859 production Boss 429s that followed, but only Mr. Knudsen's Mustang kept you cool inside the cab.

NASCAR 429

The 1969 NASCAR racing season consisted of 54 races. After a bumpy start, Ford ripped off 11 wins in a row in the summer of 1969, and David Pearson picked up the third of his three championships in a four-year window in his Holman-Moody Ford racer. The Boss 429 engine had eclipsed the 426 Hemi on the racetrack. Dodge and Plymouth responded to the shellacking by creating winged cars, but that's a story for another day.

Knudsen is Fired!

Bunkie Knudsen was called into Henry Ford II's office on September 9, 1969. Mr. Ford enjoyed winning, but he enjoyed money just a bit more. Unfortunately for Bunkie, there had been a lot of money hemorrhaging within Ford and at Kar-Kraft. A series of audits was Knudsen's downfall, as errant expenses and lost materials (parts, cars, etc.) added up.

Bunkie told the press after his dismissal, "I want to make clear today's decision, in my opinion, is unwarranted in view of the accomplishments the company has made during my brief tenure."

Bunkie wanted to win no matter the cost, but that mindset cost him his job. The snowball effect of Mr. Knudsen's firing was not known for many years, especially pertaining to an air-conditioned Boss 429.

Larry Thomas

Larry Thomas was a test technician in the road-test data-acquisition group for Ford in 1969. On September 11, 1969, Larry and his friend and coworker Bill Russo chatted about Bill's interest in purchasing a new family car. Sensing an adventure, Larry decided to accompany Bill to Ford's resale lot, where an oddity of vehicles came and went as various projects came to an end.

The resale lot opened around 8:30 a.m., so Bill and Larry got a head start and were at the gate around 8:15 a.m. It didn't take long for them to notice a line forming behind them. Bill spotted a Pinto wagon, which was the family car he was seeking and headed straight for it, while a black Mustang fastback with gold striping caught Larry's eye.

Larry proceeded to take the Mustang out on a short cruise around the resale lot. The car felt strong to him, and he really dug how different this Mustang looked versus what he saw on the street. As he idled back to the location where he began the test drive, he noticed a half-dozen individuals waiting for their turn in the Mustang. Instead of handing the keys to the next person, Larry proceeded straight to the lot manager. To the tune of $2,950, Larry became the owner of this oddball Mustang.

Larry and the Boss 429

Larry thoroughly enjoyed his new car and updated the hood scoop with a custom 429 unit. Weekend activities involved cruising Woodward Avenue and Telegraph Road as well as frequent trips to Detroit and the Milan Dragway where he ran A-Stock and dipped the

B9 into the low 13s, which was considerably faster than bone-stock Boss 429s.

At one point in late March 1970, Larry sent an internal note to Ford and asked if he could get aluminum heads installed on his Boss. However, an internal memo from Kar-Kraft dignitaries Charles Mountain, Jacque Passino, Roy Lunn, and others composed by Jim Mason outlined why it couldn't take place.

"The installation of production aluminum heads affects various other engine components," the memo stated. "When the heads are changed, it is also necessary to change the intake manifold, exhaust manifold, H-pipe, and the water outlet to [the] air conditioning. All mounting brackets and attachments are made special for this car, as no Boss 429s were built for production with air conditioning."

In summation, Larry was told, "No."

Larry's tenure lasted for a few years into the early 1970s. He eventually sold the Mustang to Sonny Hall, who later sold it to Stan Webster, a welder from Ypsilanti, Michigan.

Through conversations with Stan's brothers, Steven and Kelly, the car remained in the family until the early 1980s. Stan rebuilt it with the intention of going International Motor Sports Association (IMSA) racing.

A crowd watches Larry Thomas pace the Boss 429 at Milan Dragway. (Photo Courtesy Larry Thomas)

The Bunkie Knudsen Boss Legacy

Larry Thomas found out he owned Bunkie Knudsen's Boss 429 Mustang shortly after he purchased it. He recalled bumping into Larry Shinoda, told him about the car, and was kind of dismissed. Shinoda worked on hundreds of special cars, so hearing about one of them wasn't a big deal. He also wasn't involved in the Boss 429 program. This was Detroit. Back then, performance cars of all kinds were produced by the manufacturers. What we consider to be special today wasn't always considered special in the past.

Of those initial prototypes, only Bunkie's Boss and KK1201 have proven to exist beyond the 1970s. The 1201 car became a mule at Ford, wore multiple hats, and found its way to the resale lot. It left Ford's hands on May 6, 1969.

Had Bunkie's Boss 429 survived, it would sit atop the heap as one of the most desirable and coolest Mustangs ever built.

Stan Webster was the last confirmed owner of Bunkie's old Boss 429. It had been parked on the street before it was parted out and sent to the scrap yard. Unfortunately, that was the case with many Midwest cars that had unknown provenance in the 1970s. (Photo Courtesy Steven Webster)

1969 FORD BOSS BRONCO PROTOTYPE
By Todd Zuercher

In 1969, the Boss Bronco was photographed outside of the rotunda showroom at Ford's product development center's styling building after the application of its Boss Bronco stripes. (Photo Courtesy Colin Comer)

It was 1963, and the world didn't know it yet, but Ford would make a small four-wheel-drive vehicle that was eventually known as a sport utility vehicle (SUV). Prior to the beginning of the engineering of the vehicle, Ford conducted surveys with a group of members from four-wheel-drive clubs throughout the country. Those surveys showed that four-wheel-drive owners wanted more protection from the weather, more-refined highway manners, higher cruising speeds, a better ride, and more-powerful powertrains.

Ford delivered on all of those desires when the Bronco was introduced for the 1966 model year. Considering what the competition offered at the time, the initial 170-ci 6-cylinder engine and the 289 V-8 that soon followed delivered adequate horsepower and torque to satisfy most owners. If you wanted more power, there was always the aftermarket. As the years went by, the Bronco gained more creature

Ford Boss Vehicles

Accomplished designer Larry Shinoda made the transition to Ford Motor Company with Bunkie Knudsen in 1968. As homage to one of his mentors, Shinoda christened the name "Boss" to Kar-Kraft's NASCAR 429 Mustang that was constructed for homologation usage.

However, many Ford vehicles included the nickname across other engine packages. The 1969 Boss 429s were first, but they were not the first Fords to include the shotgun 429.

Kar-Kraft initially converted Galaxies to 429 power. Bunkie sensed the inability to sell 500 copies of a high-performance, full-size muscle car, so he instructed the brass at Kar-Kraft to use the Mustang platform instead. The Boss prevailed, and consumers had 1969 and 1970 Boss 302 and 429 Mustangs along with a 1971 351-powered variant at their disposal.

Subsequent research has revealed the following Boss-equipped cars built by Ford and its various skunkworks divisions:

- 1969 Boss 429 Galaxie
- 1969 Boss 429 Mustang
- 1969 Boss 429 Cougar
- 1969 Boss 302 Mustang
- 1969 Boss 302 Cougar Eliminator
- 1969 Boss 429 Fairlane
- 1969 Boss 351 Bronco
- 1969 Boss 302 Shelby GT350
- 1969 Boss 429 Shelby GT500
- 1969 Boss 429 Low Investment Driveline Mustang (Midship)
- 1970 Boss 429 Mustang
- 1970 Boss 429 Composite Mustang (Quarterhorse)
- 1970 Boss 302 Mustang
- 1970 Boss 302 Cougar Eliminator
- 1970 Boss 302 Maverick
- 1970 Boss 302 Maverick (Ford of Canada)
- 1970 Boss 429 Maverick
- 1970 Boss 429 Torino King Cobra
- 1970 Boss 429 Cyclone Spoiler II
- 1971 Boss 302 Mustang
- 1971 Boss 351 Mustang

Simply stated, Bossing a Ford vehicle maximized the usage of the parts bin on various models for mass-production considerations with performance in mind.

comforts and a few more conveniences. A year after its introduction, the Sport package was introduced, which brought bright trim to various body parts along with a few dress-up items for the interior.

In 1973, the Ranger model was introduced. Carpet, insulated panels, more insulation, and other niceties were added to give a modicum of luxury to what was, at its core, a very simple SUV.

Despite this variety of models and trim packages, Ford didn't have anything that resembled a high-performance model of the Bronco. Ford's work with subcontracted racing companies produced some high-performance models, most notably the Mustangs and Cobras from its partnership with Shelby American, the Boss 429s with help from Kar-Kraft, and a wide variety of racing vehicles from outfits such as Holman-Moody and Bud Moore Engineering.

Bill Stroppe

Ford had someone who knew Broncos and was familiar with making them perform well on- and off-road. That man was Bill Stroppe. Stroppe had first caught the eye of the Ford Motor Company back in 1947 when he and his partner Clay Smith put a 6-cylinder Ford pickup engine in a boat and produced spectacular results in a Detroit-area boat race. Along the way, they solved a vibration problem in the engine that had stumped the Ford engineers.

Over the next 20-plus years, Stroppe was the West Coast high-performance outlet for Ford Motor Company and took on all kinds of interesting projects for the automaker while also maintaining its press fleet. These experiences included managing the Lincoln team for the Carrera Pan America races in Mexico in the mid-1950s, running the Mercury stock-car program for many years, and claiming many victories in off-road races with the new Broncos.

How exactly Stroppe and Kar-Kraft (Ford's clandestine racing division and skunkworks) were joined for a special Bronco project in 1969 will likely never be known. In June 1969, Stroppe spent nine days at the Kar-Kraft facility in Brighton, Michigan, and helped assemble a Bronco known as the Boss Bronco.

What Stroppe and the craftsmen at Kar-Kraft created during that week in 1969 was a high-performance Bronco. It featured a combination of aftermarket parts that were proven in Stroppe's race Broncos and some careful choices from Ford's parts bin. The resulting product served as not only a vision of what a performance Bronco

Under the hood, the 1969 210S-code GT350-spec 351 Windsor power-plant was fully blueprinted at Ford before installation. The aftermarket air cleaner was likely chosen for its hood clearance. The power brake booster was a later owner-installed addition and a good idea with this much added power. (Photo Courtesy Colin Comer)

could look like in 1969 but also as a foreshadowing element of what was to come.

Shelby GT-350 Power and C4 Automatic Transmission

To address the heart of performance, the stock 302 V-8 was removed and replaced with a Kar-Kraft massaged 210S-code high-performance 351 Windsor engine from a 1969 Shelby GT-350, replete with its 4-valve induction and dual exhaust.

Stroppe could have installed a 4-speed Toploader transmission behind the 351, as he had done in countless installations in his California facility. Instead, he and Kar-Kraft performed what is believed to be the first automatic transmission swap in an early Bronco.

The adapter between the C4 transmission and the Dana 20 transfer case was clearly hand-fabricated at Kar-Kraft, but it got the job done. An auxiliary Stewart-Warner transmission oil cooler, plumbed in with Aeroquip lines and fittings, kept the transmission cool under heavy use. While an automatic seems counterintuitive from a high-performance standpoint, automatic transmissions have some advantages when off-roading, particularly when racing. On the street, an automatic can make a bucking Bronco a little easier to tame. Shifting is handled by a nicely integrated Mustang T-handle floor shifter, which helps with the high-performance vibe.

The Ride

The rest of the drivetrain was left alone. Dual shock absorbers at each corner were the height of off-road performance modifications in this era, so Stroppe added a set to this Bronco. They were standard on his race Broncos and a common aftermarket addition.

The installation of a C4 automatic transmission continued to the interior with this well-executed adaptation of a Ford passenger-car floor shifter. Note the original Bronco Sport oatmeal-colored rubber floor covering that was retained. (Photo Courtesy Colin Comer)

In the rear, the Stroppe roll bar is visible as well as the custom interior finishing panels over the rear quarter panels, the vinyl-covered wheel wells and lower tailgate, and the repurposed rocker-panel molding used to cover the inside edge of the hardtop and its mounting hardware. The Boss Bronco was a very thorough and well-thought-out build and was intended to be a top-of-the-range offering, much like a Boss Mustang. (Photo Courtesy Colin Comer)

Fiberglass rear fender cutouts were installed to give clearance for the larger tires and wheels, which consisted of 15x8 chrome steel wheels with Gates Commando tires. These were commonly used on Stroppe's builds at the time and were standard equipment on his Baja Broncos that were introduced for the 1971 model year. Factory Traction-Lok differentials front and rear with stout 4.11:1 gears ensured that the hot-rod Bronco moved with authority through any terrain.

Cab

In addition to the aforementioned Mustang floor shifter, Stroppe added a few more items to the interior. A Stroppe roll bar was added for a measure of rollover protection. The inside of the rear quarter panels, wheel wells, and tailgate were finished with custom basket-weave vinyl-covered panels. Bronco rocker-panel trim pieces were called into service to smartly finish the otherwise-exposed hardtop-mounting bolts. It was a fitting interior for an upscale, high-performance off-roading vehicle. Similar trim panels were added to the Bronco for the 1973 model year as part of the Ranger package.

The muscular stance of the high-performance Boss Bronco is hard to ignore with its Stroppe fender flares, fat 10-inch-wide wheels, and over-sized tires. If you missed those details, the racy graphics package and dual exhaust were there to remind you this was no ordinary production Bronco. (Photo Courtesy Colin Comer)

Bossing the Bronco

The exterior treatment is a story unto itself. When this truck was built, Bunkie Knudsen was running Ford Motor Company. Based on some of his favorite cars (he owned a yellow 1969 Talladega built by Kar-Kraft), a pale shade of yellow (like on this Bronco) was his favorite color. Whether the Empire Yellow paint was meant to curry Bunkie's favor to approve the project is unknown, but it certainly didn't hurt. To that end, the Special Bronco project was quickly named the "Boss Bronco."

Similar to the production Boss Mustangs, the Boss Bronco name fell in line with the Boss brand and continued Larry Shinoda's homage to his boss Bunkie Knudsen. The Boss Bronco's hockey-stick stripes resembled those on the 1969 Boss 302 Mustang as well as the Boss 351 Mustang that was built in 1971. The grille's black color treatment was a sign of things to come. It appeared later as part of the Special Décor package on the 1976–1977 Broncos. The hood scoop was plucked from Ford's high-performance Mercury Cougar Eliminator.

Unfortunately, in September 1969, Bunkie Knudsen was famously relieved of his duties at Ford by Henry Ford II. Because of that, the Boss Bronco project was done. This one and only prototype, listed on Kar-Kraft's 1969 inventory sheet as "Non-Resalable" [sic] went into storage and was destined to be scrapped. Thankfully, the Boss Bronco prototype escaped—most likely during the liquidation of Kar-Kraft in December 1970.

Found and New Ownership

Amazingly, this significant Bronco was unknown to modern-day Ford and Bronco historians until 2016, when Wes Eisenschenk found it listed as a Special Bronco on a long-lost Kar-Kraft inventory list while researching vehicles for CarTech's book on Kar-Kraft.

Some online sleuthing by Eisenschenk revealed that the truck had recently been offered for sale on eBay. How exactly the Bronco escaped the clutches of Kar-Kraft and entered the public sphere of ownership is still a mystery. It likely found its way to Ford's resale lot and was available to employees.

When Eisenschenk contacted the seller of the Bronco on eBay, it thankfully had not been sold. They were able to agree on a price, and Eisenschenk became the new owner. The prior owner's family had owned the Bronco for many decades but knew nothing of its history. They knew their late father had worked in Detroit and did something involving cars, but he suffered from Alzheimer's in his later years and was unable to fill in any blanks when they became curious about his prized truck that they only knew as the "Bumblebee Bronco."

Although the Bronco had lost its "Boss Bronco" lettering on its flanks and endured a few other changes over the years, it was remarkably original and well preserved—not to mention instantly recognizable when compared to the photos from Ford when it was new.

In November 2016, Wes sold the Boss Bronco to noted Ford and Shelby collector Colin Comer. Comer performed a sympathetic mechanical refreshment and, using Ford's original photos of the truck, recreated decals for the Bronco's flanks to return the Boss Bronco to exactly how it appeared outside of the Ford Design Center in 1969.

Ford used the Boss Bronco to help introduce the new sixth-generation (2021-and-newer) Bronco to the media at the Holly Hills Off-Road Park in Holly, Michigan, in August 2020. At the time, Ford hinted that a high-performance 6G Bronco, much like the Boss Bronco, was in the works. We now know that was the 2022 Bronco Raptor. (Photo Courtesy Colin Comer)

More than 50 years after its construction, most of which were spent hiding in plain sight, the Boss Bronco enjoys a fairly sedate existence today. It is used for events, including the Ford Motor Company's sixth-generation Bronco introduction in Detroit, and it is regularly exercised by Comer to ferry his kids to school. Most importantly, the truck continues to be conscientiously preserved with its special history restored so that future generations will always know who's the boss of the Bronco world.

Presumed to be prior to its availability on the Ford resale lot, the Boss Bronco is parked in front of what appears to be a bank in Detroit. If this location looks familiar, please reach out to the author. (Photo Courtesy Colin Comer)

1969 FORD BOSS 429 MUSTANG LOW INVESTMENT DRIVELINE

By Charlie Henry

A Mach 1 donor car served as the template for the Low Investment Driveline (LID) prototype. (Photo Courtesy Ford Motor Company)

In the early 1960s, Ford began building its high-performance image. The objective was to improve sales. While the performance of its domestic cars was improved with engines including the 390, 406, and 427, Henry "the Deuce" Ford II wanted global recognition. To that end, he declared that Ford would race internationally. The company entered discussions to buy Ferrari and have a ready-made, competitive race team. Enzo Ferrari backed out at the last minute, which infuriated Henry Ford. He vowed to go to war and beat Ferrari at his own game and win the 24 Hours of Le Mans endurance race.

To race at Le Mans, Ford had to assemble a shop, a team of engineers, and a race car from scratch. Since corporate red tape and regular production engineering needs hindered the free-wheeling way of designing, building, and racing an internationally competitive car, an outside shop was brought in. That shop was Kar-Kraft, an independently owned company that was contracted exclusively to Ford. It had the facilities and engineers to do the job.

The first task was to create the mid-engine GT40, which first raced at Le Mans in 1964. The car was devilishly fast but did not finish the race. Several versions followed, as Ford and Kar-Kraft engineers revised and upgraded the car. The final two versions, the Mk II and the Mk IV, soundly beat the Ferraris and won in 1966 and 1967, respectively. An entertaining and fairly accurate account of the war can be seen in the 2019 film *Ford v Ferrari*.

Once Ford won Le Mans, Kar-Kraft's main job was done, but Ford was not done with the company. The engineers and facilities proved to be a fast, responsive, and versatile asset. Ford started to direct special projects to Kar-Kraft. Among those projects was the Mach 2 experimental sports-car prototype, the production Boss 302 Mustang, the Boss 302 Mustang Trans-Am race cars, the Boss 429 Mustang, the Torino Talladega, a four-wheel-drive Mustang, a mid-engine Can-Am race car, and a Lincoln armored presidential limousine. These are a few of the many projects Ford sent to Kar-Kraft.

The development of the Mach 2 experimental sports car used a 1967 Mustang convertible as a donor car with a 289-ci engine and rear suspension that mimicked a GT40. In total, three cars were produced and evolved the prototype into Mach 2 A, B, and C forms. The concept was dropped, as the new 1969 Mustang bodies were a significant departure from the current platform. The cancellation of the Mach 2 paved the way for the Low Investment Driveline (LID) 1969 Mustang.

The mid-engine Mach 2 was intended to be a stand-alone sports car in the Ford Cobra–style vein. (Photo Courtesy Jim Mason)

Mid-Engine

The idea of a mid-engine Mustang was possibly inspired by the Boss 429 production program. Shoehorning the Boss engine into the engine bay of a regular Mustang was problematic. The engine was too wide to fit between the shock towers on the side aprons of the engine bay. The solution was to replace the stock towers with new, modified aprons and shock towers. The stock aprons were not modified or welded at the Boss 429 Brighton assembly plant. The new panels were installed on the Rouge production line in place of the stock aprons. Even with the new aprons, the engine was still a tight fit. The engine installation required special procedures that could not be done on the Rouge line.

There were several thoughts behind the idea of installing a rear-mounted engine:

- Room for any size of engine (the Boss 429, 428 Cobra Jet, 429 Cobra Jet, 429 Super Cobra Jet, 302, and the upcoming 351)

Seeing a Boss 429 on an assembly cradle is an impressive sight. It is even more impressive to fit it under the rear glass of the Mach 1. (Photo Courtesy Ford Motor Company)

- Better weight distribution for improved traction and handling
- Develop low-cost or LID components from inventory or vendors when necessary
- Provide a top-of-the-line, somewhat-exotic performance car
- Estimate costs of designing, testing, certifying, and production

The project was given the go-ahead in 1968 with a speculated production date target of 1971½. Kar-Kraft pulled a stock 1969 Mustang Mach 1 from the Rouge assembly plant and cut out the trunk floor. The engineers designed a subframe, or cradle, that held the engine, transmission, differential, and suspension. It was a clever package that was easily installed or removed. No bodywork was necessary to clear the big F-60x15 Polyglas tires. The gas tank moved to the right-hand rear inner fender. The filler was hidden behind the fake scoop on the outside of the fender. The Boss 429 engine needed no modifications.

From the rear, the cockpit of the now-two-seater Mach 1 is visible through the glass divider. The Boss 429 snorkel was shortened for clearance. (Photo Courtesy Ford Motor Company)

Adaptation

Both the engine and C-6 automatic transmission sat backward in the subframe and faced the rear of the car. A purpose-designed cast transfer case replaced the regular C-6 output housing. This case turned the output shaft 180 degrees to direct power along the engine toward the rear of the car.

A standard Ford 9-inch nodular-iron differential and housing attached to a special casting that held the engine mounts and suspension pickup points. The subframe positioned the differential assembly under and to one side of the engine. Kar-Kraft modified the differential housing to fit the application and accept individual driveshafts in place of traditional axle shafts. The rear suspension was independent with coilover shock absorbers to hold up the car. With this design, the engine sat directly over the rear axle. The Mustang's weight distribution changed from 60-percent front and 40-percent rear to 40-percent front and 60-percent rear.

The battery, radiator, and air-conditioning condenser remained in the former front engine bay. An electric fan helped move air through the stock radiator. Rather than go to the expense of fancy aftermarket wheels (since the car was an engineering exercise and not a show car), the front wheels were plain steel. The rear wheels were also steel, but the center section was offset to fit the new suspension and driveshaft and to center the tire in the fender well. Lincoln full-wheel covers gave the car a finished appearance.

Apart from the missing rear seat, the interior changed little. A vertical panel that separated the cockpit from the transmission replaced the seat back. A vertical glass window was fitted atop the panel and provided rear visibility and a view of the engine. The area behind the bucket seats was covered with carpeting to match the existing stock floor carpet. The throttle pedal was not relocated—it just had a longer cable to reach the engine. The floor-mounted shifter remained in place and functioned the same. The rear window glass was removed for access to the engine. A set of the optional Mustang Sport Slats covered the window opening and acted as an engine cover and engine ventilator.

The LID Mustang was a success as a proof-of-concept exercise. It met all the targets and answered all the questions. The mid-engine and transmission installation could be done with a minimum of fabricated parts. Body modifications were not complicated, and the installation was reasonable in terms of production. The new weight distribution nearly eliminated wheelspin and did not upset drivability. In fact, most drivers, including both engineers and non-engineers, found it difficult to tell the difference between the front- and mid-mounted cars.

Although the project was successful, the LID Mustang died. There were no reasonable justifications or advantages to produce the car. Marketing a semi-exotic car that performed no better than existing cars would be difficult, if not ineffective. Stocking repair and service parts for a limited production car would create an expensive burden for dealers. Corporate budget cuts, along with the end of Kar-Kraft's contract, sealed the car's fate.

Most concept, experimental, and prototype vehicles were destroyed at the end of their program. Without a VIN or title, and with uncertifiable modifications or parts, the cars were not salable. The LID fit that category and was scheduled for the shredder. End of story.

However, no records exist of it actually being destroyed. It simply disappeared. Not even the engineers and technicians who worked on it know its fate. As often happens with such cars, rumors abound: It was spirited out of the impound area. The body shell is somewhere on the western side of Michigan. The engine, transaxle, and cradle are in a private garage in the Detroit area.

Even if the car and components were found, reassembling them would be difficult, if not impossible. There was an engine/transmission/cradle display unit, in addition to the unit in the car, but that display unit was a shell. There were no guts in the engine, transfer case, or transaxle. There are no spare parts lying around. All the unused castings were discarded. Blueprints were lost or destroyed with the closure of Kar-Kraft. All the people who worked on the project are gone.

The LID Mustang is fated to be a small footnote in the performance history of Ford Motor Company.

1969 PONTIAC TRANS AM PROTOTYPES

By Wes Eisenschenk

This publicity shot showcases one of the 1969 Trans Am prototypes. It was likely taken in California near the time of the Riverside debut. (Photo Courtesy General Motors)

Typically, the words "Trans Am" create visions of Bo "the Bandit" Darville blazing through the Alabama countryside with Buford T. Justice in hot pursuit. Others likely recall a talking 1982 Trans Am named "KITT" (Knight Industries Two Thousand) having idle conversations with his crime-fighting pilot, Michael Knight, while they attempt to capture the day's favorite bad guy. But, how many of us think of those 697 Pontiac Trans Ams that made up the manufacturers first-year run of performance-oriented pony cars? For that story, we must start at the beginning.

The Trans Am's heritage dates back to 1967 with the Pontiac Firebird Sprint Turismo (PFST). It all started when John DeLorean grew a bit tired of the Chevrolet Camaro SS outpacing the Firebird in the performance image department. After DeLorean had been defeated by GM brass in bringing a two-seater Pontiac Banshee into the marketplace to rival the Corvette, he cast his gaze at the rival Camaro SS. The PFST was his first step of evolving the softly successful Firebird into the image killer that he envisioned for Pontiac.

1969½

In 1969, every manufacturer found a new booster to inject into its midyear production models. Mopar offered 440-6 Road Runners and Super Bees. The Blue Oval had its slippery Ford Talladegas and Mercury Cyclone Spoilers. Oldsmobile circumvented the over-400-ci-displacement ban with its Hurst/Olds. Even AMC sent its little Rambler out in style with the SC/Rambler. In his own office, DeLorean spiced up the GTO with the Judge package. The midyear Trans Am was right at home in the hurried sales push of March 1969.

On tracks across America, every manufacturer dumped money into its research and development departments to make go-fast parts for racing. Across NASCAR, NHRA, and Trans-Am racing, specialty-built race cars battled on the circuits while their homologation counterparts tore up the streets.

DeLorean knew that if his new Trans Am was going to put the proverbial dent into the competitors' sales numbers, it better walk the walk to back up the talk.

Trans Am, What's Your Pleasure?

DeLorean instructed his styling division to contact none other than customizer royalty Gene Winfield. The Firebird was in the last year of its model cycle (1967–1969), and Winfield was asked to enhance the car. In early 1968, Gene received engineering drawings and classified photos as a general baseline for the car. Winfield contracted well-known artist Terry Bradley to work on some renderings for the secret "Can-Am" project at Pontiac. By June 1968, Winfield submitted his proposals to Pontiac's styling department, which provided the go-ahead for developmental work on the custom touches that adorned the Firebird that served as the Trans Am prototype.

Winfield converted the approved sketches that were greenlit for concept development into working fiberglass prototypes. Gene sent them to Detroit and was flown in for a six-day stay. Gene was in the process of applying them onto the prototype when DeLorean strolled in at Pontiac's production engineering department. He walked around the car to inspect the unique touches and approved six of the seven modifications that Winfield created for the car. These included the handcrafted dual-scoop hood, front brake ducts, fender-mounted air extractors, and a large rear spoiler. An extension at the base of the hood that concealed the windshield wipers was rejected.

After approval, Winfield painted the molds to match the Palladium Silver paint on the 1969 Firebird and created the first Pontiac Trans Am. DeLorean came back the next day to see the final product, was smitten with Gene's creation, and put his next efforts into powering the Trans Am.

Under the special hood that was steel framed with fiberglass skin, the prototype received the potent Ram Air IV 400-ci engine that pumped out an underrated 345 hp. Both this engine and the Ram Air III 400-ci with 335 hp was available in production Trans Am units. The prototype featured an automatic transmission, but both an automatic and 4-speed were available from the factory.

Finalizing the build, Pontiac's styling studio took Winfield's rear spoiler and refined it, as the special-projects department wanted maximum downforce with the least amount of drag. The department made adjustments and test runs for a week with one of the 1968 PFST cars as a mule. The sweet spot came with the spoiler that created 100 pounds of downforce at 100 mph. The prototype wore Rally II wheels with F70-14 whitewall tires.

Showtime

In November 1968, three Trans Ams were shipped to California to be featured in magazines. *Hot Rod, Car Life,* and *Autoweek* had content in their March 1969 issues.

Steve Kelly of *Hot Rod* put the Trans Am through its paces while complimenting and critiquing the car's performance and aesthetics. Praise was given to the car's handling and interior finishing with negative marks reported on the Trans Am name decals and an overall disdain for the 1969 Firebird's styling.

A trip to Orange County Raceway was next on the agenda where the Trans Am was put through its paces. Rolling on the F70-14s with 45 psi up front and 32 psi on the rears, the prototype made a 14.10-second pass at 100.78 mph. The only modifications to the car were adjusting the timing to 39 degrees and putting in a set of 0.030-gapped AC 44S resistors.

Kelly concluded the session with the prototype and noted, "If a car that goes around bends, curves, hairpins, pylons, or mountains better than or as good as it goes quarter-miling is something that the

From the rear, the 1969 Trans Am looked like a boulevard bruiser. It would be interesting to see how sales could have been affected had the car been offered in silver, as opposed to white with blue stripes. (Photo Courtesy General Motors)

people of the world have been waiting for, then it's here. If not, it's here anyway, and we enjoyed telling you about it."

Being that it was a prototype and not a finished production version of a Trans Am may have played a role in Kelly's demeanor about the aesthetics.

Ron Hickman of *Competition Press* and *Autoweek* drove the silver 4-speed car in Las Vegas at Stardust International Raceway where he noted the car "stuck like glue" on the corners of the racetrack. The March 22, 1969, review also recorded a 14.69 ET at 99.44 mph and a top speed of 135-plus-mph on the desert highway, all with a 3.90 gear ratio.

Introducing the Trans Am

On December 8, 1968, at Riverside International Raceway in Riverside, California, the all-new Trans Am and 1969 GTO Judge were revealed to the awaiting automotive press. In total, three Trans Ams are believed to have made their debut at this event: our feature car, another Palladium Silver Ram Air IV 4-speed machine, and a Cameo White Ram Air T/A car with blue stripes.

The Michigan license plates for these cars were as follows:

- RAIV 4-speed: 10M-249
- RAIV automatic: 10M-216
- RAIII: GM-2958

Where Did They Go?

Things start to get a little fuzzy after the Trans Am's debut in California. The brigade of magazine stories fizzled out after March 1969, and the 10M-249 car was invoiced to Royal Pontiac in Hollywood, California. Perhaps it never left California after the December tests.

Trans-Am series regular Jerry Titus purchased the 10M-249 car and used it for aero testing and daily driving duties. He sold it in 1970, and it stayed in California for the next 30 years. The car was found on eBay in 2009 and purchased by Curt Richards. It made its debut at the 2014 MCACN event and sold at Barrett-Jackson in 2015 for $313,500.

The 10M-216 vehicle has not been seen since the testing session in Nevada.

It's unclear if the GM-2958 car returned to Michigan for further development.

The Pontiac Trans Am was deemed a huge success for the manufacturer. The car always maintained a performance image over its sister car, the Firebird. These three unique Trans Ams each offered a glimpse into what could be Pontiac's greatest creation of all-time. Thank you, John DeLorean.

GM-2958 poses for publicity shots on a winding road in rural California. (Photo Courtesy MotorTrend)

1970 FORD BOSS MAVERICK PROTOTYPES

By Wes Eisenschenk

The Boss 302 Maverick poses for internal photos at Ford. With its chin spoiler, custom C-stripe, and domed hood, the Maverick had quite a different presence compared to its Mustang stablemate. (Photo Courtesy Ford Motor Company)

By now, we've all heard that 1970 was the high-water mark for the muscle car. Due to automotive regulations, manufacturers that produced high-output engines received smog- and emissions-related hurdles to overcome. How did the manufacturers respond? They did so by creating some of the nastiest small-block muscle cars ever.

In 1950, Nash built the first compact automobile. An executive at Nash coined the term "compact" to describe a car with a wheelbase of 110 inches or less. Other manufacturers followed the Nash Rambler's lead with automobiles such as the Hudson Jet, Willys Aero, and Kaiser-Frazer Henry J.

By the beginning of the 1960s, nearly everyone had a compact, as the Ford Falcon, Chevrolet Corvair, Plymouth Valiant, and Studebaker Lark entered the market and solidified a new class of automobile.

Enter the Pony Car

Just as the compact began to take a noticeable slice of the pie from the mid- and full-size market, along came the pony car. Plymouth and Ford repackaged their Valiant and Falcon platforms to offer the Barracuda and Mustang. While steady sales continued for the compacts, the aggressive look of the pony car became an inviting place to add performance.

Compacts Respond

In 1963, Studebaker was the first to take a stab at performance with its R2 supercharged 289 with 289 hp. Chevrolet's Chevy II, built to compete against the Falcon, followed suit with its 1965 327-ci V-8 Turbo-Fire, which was the first compact to crest the 300-hp barrier. The horsepower wars were inevitably found across all U.S. production lines, as each abandoned the original reason for the compact.

However, just like a stretched rubber band, the demise of the muscle car brought back the compacts in a big way.

While some nameplates forged through the muscle-car era intact and on the same platform (the Nova, Dart, and Valiant), others traversed onto other bodystyles (the Falcon and Comet) or ended up on the cutting-room floor (the Corvair and Rambler). Lastly, new compacts (the Maverick and Hornet) debuted and were joined by a new class called the subcompact (the Gremlin, Vega, and Pinto).

Ford Maverick

Ford's Falcon nameplate adorned six compact and midsize models and now shared a body with the Torino for 1970, so the two-door Maverick debuted as a direct competitor to the Dart and Nova and started under $2,000.

It debuted in April 1969, and the Maverick had a running start for the 1970 model year. Ultimately, 578,914 units were sold compared to 254,242 Novas and 210,104 Darts, outselling Chevrolet and Dodge compacts combined. Even with so much market saturation, Ford considered battling the performance models of the Nova and Dart for a brief second.

Ford Boss Vehicles

Created for homologation purposes to get Ford's new engine into NASCAR, the Boss 429 was the first Ford to utilize Larry Shinoda's "Boss" nickname for Ford President Bunkie Knudsen on one of its cars. Boss 429s were developed and built at a Ford-for-hire location.

Soon to follow was the Boss 302, a Trans-Am racer that needed homologation copies created for that sanctioning series. Although the Boss 302 was developed at Kar-Kraft, Ford handled the mass production of the street copies. Other 1969 Fords that saw Kar-Kraft prototype and developmental work and used the Boss name were the Cougar, Galaxie, and Bronco models.

Kar-Kraft

Derived as a skunkworks operation for Ford in the mid-1960s, Kar-Kraft was most known for creating the GT40s and for Boss 429 production. However, Ford kept the staff at Kar-Kraft consistently busy with other side projects for development and manufacturing. From prototype work to special projects, Kar-Kraft grew throughout the 1960s and included seven locations where various projects were under development.

Boss 302 Maverick

For 1970, Ford dug into the Boss nameplate again and assigned the moniker to the Maverick. With the Mustang and Cougar lines still utilizing the Boss 302 engine (the Boss 429 was used on the Mustang only for 1970), Ford took a peek behind the curtain regarding what a Boss 302 Maverick street fighter looked like.

The Maverick and Mustang shared a similar engine compartment that allowed for the Boss 302 to be transplanted with relative ease. Aesthetically, the car was visually similar to a production-model Grabber car but included a white-painted hood and cowl top (production Grabbers were black), white C-stripe, chrome driver's side mirror, chin spoiler, and "BOSS" graphics above the Maverick fender logos.

Just a handful of images exist of the Boss 302 Maverick, and it's unclear if the car was a shade of blue or green, or if multiple experimental cars were created.

Behind Kar-Kraft's Haggerty Street shop, the Boss Maverick poses with the 1967 Mach 2 in the background. This was likely the last photo ever taken of the car. (Photo Courtesy Jim Mason)

Boss 429 Maverick

The Boss 302 Maverick that was conceived and created by Kar-Kraft spawned the ultimate machine: the Boss 429 Maverick. A hemihead 429 was shoehorned into the dainty Maverick and created an

With a manufacturer's license plate installed, the Boss 429 appears to rest after a night of prowling Woodward Avenue. A pair of 1970 Cougar Eliminators, Ed Terry's drag Mustang, and a late-model Fairlane keep the Maverick company. (Photo Courtesy Jim Mason)

instant street weapon that could leave any Yenko or Hemi car blushing.

It's unclear if the Boss 429 Maverick was strictly a feasibility test vehicle or if it was utilized for offering over-the-counter parts purchasing. Either the car was built to see if the 429 fit in a Maverick or (if it did fit) was used to see how the parts worked. What is clear is that with its sinister snorkel, roll cage, and Goodyear slicks, it was taillight city for anyone who thought Mavericks were pushovers.

Canadian Colt Boss 302 Maverick

Not to be outdone by its American counterpart, Ford of Canada pursued the feasibility of producing a Boss 302 Maverick. Nicknamed "the Colt," the special performance department took an aggressive approach to its version of a Boss Maverick. Created under John Philipps's advisement, the Colt featured Grabber Orange paint, a black C-stripe, shaker hood, Boss 302 decals, a blacked-out hood treatment on the cowl and rear deck, hood pins, front and rear spoilers, and an orange-blaze striped interior.

The Colt debuted at the 1970 Ford of Canada Racer's Banquet in Toronto alongside the Sandy Elliot race team, Beatty and Woods, and other racers.

Performance-wise, the Colt had a blueprinted Boss 302 with a Sig Erson cam, an automatic transmission out of a 351 Mustang, a Winters 3,000-stall modified torque converter, 9-inch Traction-Lok rear

Not to be outdone by its American counterpart, Ford of Canada produced the Colt Boss 302 Maverick. The outlandish color, shaker hood, and rear and chin spoilers provided a menacing appearance. (Photo Courtesy Ford of Canada)

axle with a 4.30:1 ratio, Mustang sway bar, heavy-duty shocks and springs, Cragar SS mags, G70x14 Polyglas tires, 1969 Torino 428 front brakes, and 1969 Mustang GT rear brakes.

Philipps had his wife, Lynda Pleva-Philipps, stretched the Colt out at Cayuga 1320 Dragway in the summer of 1970. On street tires, the car was said to have run consistent 14.30 ETs. On slicks, it dipped into the 12.74 range.

The Colt was listed in a series of classified ads in 1971 and never heard from again.

Bossing Mavericks

It didn't take long for the general public to create its own unique variants of the Boss Maverick. A November 3, 1970, classified advertisement in *The World News* from Roanoke, Virginia, listed a 1970 Maverick with a Boss 302 and a 4-speed as a "one of a kind" vehicle that was available at Vinton Motor Co. By 1971, some dealerships were likely testing the waters on one-off builds.

Boss Maverick Legacy

What transpired after the Maverick debuted was that drag racers saw a newer, smaller platform to hot rod. Wheelmen Hubert Platt, "Fast" Eddie Schartman, Dick Brannan, Ed Skelton, "Dyno" Don Nicholson, and

'71 MAVERICK BOSS

Boss 302 V-8 engine, close ratio 4-sp. with Hurst Competition Linkage, Hurst Competition and Shifter, 4.11 rear axle ratio, 800 CFM Holley double pumper carburetor, tuned headers, Ram air system, Hurst, Comp. front shocks, Hoosier Sprint Special rear tires.

MK1-759, Serial #0K91U277585.

Griswold & Wight Ford in Modesto, California, offered this 1971 Maverick Boss 302 as a new vehicle under its demonstrator sale on April 30, 1971. No, the VIN didn't come back as registered. (Photo Courtesy Modesto Bee)

a host of others transformed the mundane Maverick into a strip killer, as Pro Stock entered a new era.

Today, the Ford Maverick nameplate has been reinvented and applied to a pickup body. Most remember it for being a sales success in the compact lineup, but some of us remember the Maverick for what it could have been: the boss of all Boss muscle cars.

1970 FORD BOSS MUSTANG 429: THE *LAWMAN*

By Wes Eisenschenk

*The imposing stance of the **Lawman** Boss 429 is on display in the evening sun. Clearance was at a minimum with the impressive powerplant under the hood. (Photo Courtesy Jeff Koch/**Hemmings Motor News**)*

Elton (Al) "The Lawman" Eckstrand had a brief career in sanctioned drag racing, but the impact that he and his cars had still resonates to this day.

A native of Detroit, Michigan, Elton received a master's degree in psychology and a doctorate degree in law. In 1955, he was hired by Chrysler and worked in the organizational department. Engaged by the local hot-rod scene in Detroit, Eckstrand climbed the ladder on the street and at the strip in a pair of Furys (1957 and 1958) and took class honors at the NHRA Nationals in Detroit driving his parents' station wagon.

In 1960, Eckstrand piloted a Chrysler 300F, backed by the division in what is considered to be one of the first factory-supported race cars. Eckstrand ran a Dodge at the U.S. Nationals in 1961—this time at Indy.

By 1962, Elton was behind the wheel of a 413 Dodge Dart and took home top honors in Super Stock at the U.S. Nationals. It was in this drag racing season that Elton became "Al" at the drag strip, separating his lawyer and drag-racing personas.

Al's next three years cemented his legacy as a Mopar wheelman.

The *Lawman*

Al won Mr. Stock Eliminator in a Ramchargers Dodge at the NHRA Winternationals in 1963 and was runner-up at the U.S. Nationals in his *Lawman* Dodge.

In January 1964, Al and Chrysler tested an altered-wheelbase 1964 Plymouth that broke ground for what became the Funny Car category. During a testing session at Lions Drag Strip, Al drove a 426 Hemi that rode atop a frame that was moved forward 2 inches and ushered in the A/FX category. Both the Hemi and the 2-percent Mopars (a total of four were constructed) had never seen a drag strip until this testing session.

Although the 2-percenters wouldn't be ready for the Winternationals, they would soon change the sport of drag racing, forever.

Eckstrand would volley between running the A/FX and S/S Plymouths for 1964 and would be a hired gun for the Golden Commandos in 1965. With the Commandos he match-raced across the country against other A/FX cars. Al's last recorded race was in September 1965, and he defeated Don Nicholson at Motor City Dragway with a 9.62 ET at 143.08 mph. Eckstrand promptly hung up his helmet and established his law firm.

Safety for Servicemen

Al's law practice didn't stand a chance once he was offered the opportunity to head the American Commandos drag racing team in 1966. Chrysler supplied Al with a new 1966 Hemi Charger that was shipped to England and the Santa Pod Raceway. There, he became Chrysler's mouthpiece for introducing automotive safety for the servicemen once they returned stateside.

For six weeks, Al gave rides and performed demonstrations on and off the track with a Dark Turquoise Metallic and White 1966 Charger along with his personal 1948 Anglia with Larry Arnold behind the controls. With the ever-growing performance of vehicles in the blossoming muscle-car industry, Al saw the need for implementing

The cavalcade of the American Commandos Racing Team lines up for a multi-manufacturer blast down the strip in the United Kingdom. (Photo Courtesy Tord Jönsson)

seminars for the overseas GIs, as there had been increases in automotive casualties.

Everything went so well for Al in England that for 1967, Chrysler set him up with a 1967 Barracuda for his encore. However, this time Al also had a partnership with Ford and showcased Mustangs as well. In total, Al had two Barracudas, two Mustangs, and a 1967 Corvette at his disposal with the American Commandos drag racing team. Who says that Mopars, Fords, and Chevrolets can't get along?

The years 1968 and 1969 saw Al in Europe as he renovated castles and captured the Sweden Drag Racing Championship. With the Vietnam War now in full swing, Al was determined that it was more critical than ever to educate servicemen on auto safety. Ironically, in 1968, there were 16,592 soldier casualties in the Vietnam War. Back home in 1969, there were 16,411 serious accidents that involved government vehicles. These were statistics that Al wanted to improve.

1970 Military Performance Tour

The Department of Defense approached Al about taking on his longest tour (4.5 months) in 1970. Al revisited his long-standing relationship with Chrysler, but it declined to be involved this time. Al's next call was to Ford, which had provided cars for the 1967 campaign. Company President Bunkie Knudsen had been ramping up

Ford's image across a myriad of platforms and happily obliged Eckstrand's request to be a part of the program.

Around $150,000 was needed for the tour, and Al secured funds from Ford, Goodyear Tire and Rubber Co., Motor Wheel Corp., Hurst Products Co., Fram Corp., B&M Transmissions, and a few others. In August 1970, Al told Hugh McCann of the *Detroit Free Press*, "By and large, they went along with the idea of promoting safety and had no ulterior motives as far as sales were concerned."

With funding intact and a manufacturer at his disposal, it was time to set up the details of the tour. The western tour commenced in February 1970 and concluded at the end of May of the same year. A second European tour began in August.

Mustangs

A total of 14 Ford Mustangs (12 production models and 2 Super Boss cars) were utilized for the tour, with 6 going to Asia and 6 to Europe. The two Super Boss cars divided time between international

Five Cobra Jet Mach 1s are parked near the Lawman *Mustang after its arrival in East Asia. (Photo Courtesy Bill Goldberg Archives)*

and domestic duties. The first swing of the international tour was full, with stops in Hawaii, South Korea, the Philippines, Guam, South Vietnam, and Japan.

The six factory-production Mach 1 428 Cobra Jet–powered Mustangs were sent to Roy Steffe Enterprises in Fairhaven, Michigan, to add some aesthetic and performance necessities. The Mach 1s were adorned with Motor Wheel Spyder mags on Goodyear rubber, Hooker headers, and a Sun tachometer. Each car received custom paint work with the lower body color matched to the hood stripe and rear decklid. That same color encased the side glass and projected forward as a single stripe atop the fenders.

The Super Boss

As entertaining and informative as the Mach 1s were, for the soldiers, the main course was the Lawman's Super Boss.

Ignited by a 1,000-hp Boss 429 with a supercharger, the Super Boss was everything that its name evoked. Converted by Roy Steffe Enterprises, two identically prepared 1970 Z-code B9s with Ford's trusty C-6 automatic transmission were created to mesmerize and educate the troops. Once they were on location, Al gauged what could be performed with the Super Boss based on how much real estate that he had to work with. Sometimes it was an airport runway, and other times it was on an aircraft carrier.

With one car overseas and the other in the U.S. (appeasing the domestic GIs), all seemed well until the international Mustang had a freak accident.

During transport on rough seas, a crate dislodged from its placement aboard a vessel and landed directly on top of the Super Boss. The unfortunate circumstance was resolved quickly when the domestic Super Boss was expedited to the next international location. It's alleged that the fate of the crushed Boss was a burial at sea.

Europe

After the Pacific theater's military performance tour concluded, Al and the team came back to the States, freshened up, and headed east for a tour of the United Kingdom, Sweden, and Germany.

A new fleet of 1970 Mach 1s joined the domestic (now international) Super Boss for a sweeping tour on the other side of the Atlantic

The European swing for the American Commando Racing Team brought the Lawman and crew to Sweden. Here, some dockworkers check out the Mustang after it was unloaded. (Photo Courtesy Starta and Speed Magazine)

Ocean. On this expedition, a Triumph 650-cc motorcycle was added to the docket.

"With the growing popularity of motorcycles in the States, it is time for a positive program about safety in motorcycle riding," Al told the *Birmingham Evening Mail* in August 1970.

Hundreds of thousands of soldiers eventually laid their eyes on these Mustangs and were educated by the seminars that Al and his team created. Al told the *Lansing State Journal* in September 1970, "Some of these kids [servicemen] got so emotional at seeing a car from home [that] they actually shed tears as they ran their hands over the cars and inspected the motors."

1971, 1972, and Beyond

Al and Ford continued the program in 1971 with a pair of Mavericks, Mustangs, and Pintos. A final tour in 1972 had a pair of Mavericks and Pintos. Although they weren't the ground-pounding the Cobra Jets and Super Bosses, education for safer driving always remained Al's first priority when on tour.

Super Boss Back Home

The sole remaining Super Boss Mustang wasn't on the later tours, but it did finally find its way to the drag strip. After returning to the U.S. in the fall of 1970, the Super Boss was stripped of its blower and sold to racer Dave McCormick, who piloted the car under the moniker *Blue Devil*.

After McCormick's passing, it was none other than Elton "Al" Eckstrand (he came back to the States in the 1990s) who wound up with the beloved B9. Al restored the Super Boss back to how it was campaigned and enjoyed his prized mount before he let it go to the next caretaker at Barrett-Jackson in 2003. Al passed away in 2008 at age 79 after a short illness.

The new caretaker was the only person capable of exhibiting the same brute force and explosiveness that the Super Boss routinely displayed: professional wrestler Bill Goldberg.

Goldberg's eclectic car collection houses some of the greatest muscle cars ever assembled in Detroit. With Hemis, Shelbys, and Yenkos, Bill's fully capable of "wrasslin" the wheel when putting these brutes through their paces. However, the champ met his match when he sat behind the wheel of the Super Boss.

In 2020, 50 years after its original debut, Mustang expert and restorer Marcus Anghel of Anghel Restorations completed a meticulous ground-up full restoration on the *Lawman* Super Boss using original photos and documentation to bring it back to its original and magnificent glory. To see it is one thing, but to hear it is a whole different experience. With some planned limited showings, Bill hopes to share this experience with many others in the upcoming years.

Scan this QR code for more information about the Super Boss.

Rear tow straps, the parachute, header pipes, and an on/off fuel switch top off the Lawman's *attire. (Photo Courtesy Jeff Koch/Hemmings Motor News)*

1970 CHRYSLER 300-H CONVERTIBLE

By Trev Dellinger

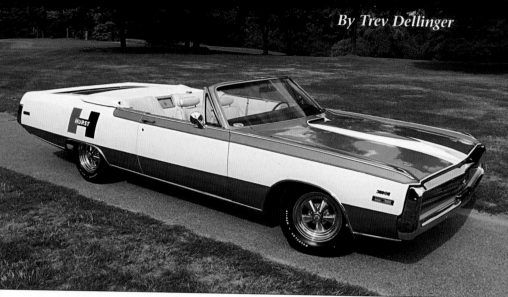

George Hurst had this 1970 Chrysler 300-H created for marketing purposes at racetracks and Hurst-related events. (Photo Courtesy Trev Dellinger)

"Better a diamond with a flaw than a pebble without."
Confucius

Seriously? Am I reading a story on an extremely rare and seldom-seen Mopar muscle car starting with a quote from Confucius? You sure are. Sometimes, things in life are more layered than they seem. The story usually has more depth and details. What we think we know is what we have been told. What we think we know is what we have heard over and over until it's either assumed as fact or becomes so mundane that it's rarely questioned.

As Confucius says, it's better to have a diamond with a flaw, and the 1970 Chrysler 300-H is one of those diamonds. It's one of those cars where most Mopar fanatics think they know the story. However, this is not to blame anyone. Why would someone question if there is more to these cars than meets the eye, especially when people say, "All [Chrysler] 300 Hursts look the same" or "If you've seen one, you've seen them all." We've all heard it hundreds of times. However, that is not the case with this diamond. Let's take a new look at this flawed diamond, the 1970 300-H convertible, and see what has been forgotten or glossed over since its inception.

Hurst Performance

Jim Wangers, Dick Chrysler, and Dave Landrith of Hurst Performance Research sat down in late 1969 and thought it would be a plausible idea to reintroduce the concept of the letter car back into the market with Chrysler's new fuselage design and use the Chrysler 300 as the base platform. The idea was to build a new letter car for the 1970s with help from Hurst. The 300-H factory literature stated, "From this legacy has been created the newest model of the famed Chrysler 300 letter-car series . . . the unique 1970 Chrysler 300-H."

Dick Maxwell, a Chrysler product engineer, is quoted in the April 1970 issue of *Motor Trend*.

"What we've done here [with the Hurst] is to take all our good options and package them," Maxwell said.

This included all of the heavy-duty options that Chrysler had for suspension, brakes, exhaust, the engine, and the transmission. In addition to those goodies, Goodyear Polyglas H70 RWL tires were part of the A12/Hurst package.

Creating the 300-H

The concept for the 300-H included a special fiberglass custom-designed power-bulge hood with an air scoop that vented into the cabin. A custom-designed fiberglass decklid with a recessed air foil/ spoiler integrated with the rear fender extensions. The rear spoiler actually functioned, as the Hurst factory owner's manual stated that it is to "create downforce at high road speeds." The custom pinstriping decals made by 3M were hand-applied rather than hand-painted, according to the manual. Unique Hurst paint was used, and 300-H/ Hurst emblems were mounted on the hood so that everyone knew what they were sitting next to at the stoplight.

Powering the H

Hurst Performance Research wanted to install the 426 Hemi engine and a Hurst Auto-Stick automatic slap-stick shifter as part of the package. But as the cars were already late into the 1970 production cycle, these items unfortunately were canceled. Chrysler mandated the 440 TNT engine with 375 hp and 485 ft-lbs of torque. The Hurst Auto-Stick shifter was scrapped as being too difficult and time consuming to install, so a column shifter was standard equipment, and the console shifter was optional. Projected production was an optimistic 2,000 units, but only 485 or 501 cars were built, depending on which records you read. That extra car in the 500 total is the 300-H promotional convertible.

Hurst 'Vert

This convertible was ordered by Hurst to promote the 300-H hardtop models. It's unknown exactly who ordered the car at Hurst, but it was ordered in the exact Hurst colors as the 1969 Hurst/Olds promotional cars. George Hurst specifically liked the white/black and gold paint, and this car was specifically ordered that way. It's logical to assume Mr. Hurst ordered the car the way he wanted it.

The 300-H convertible is a Q-code, public-relations, special-order car. It was ordered with a white top, white standard-300 bucket-seat interior, a black dash, black carpet, search-tune AM/FM radio, power seats, power windows, and more. It's a fully loaded executive muscle machine.

It's the only 300-H, or 300-Hurst as they are commonly called today, with that color scheme.

The paint on the promotional convertible differs from the standard production 300-H as well. The exterior of the convertible 300-H is a custom white, and the gold accents are Hurst Gold, which was what all the promotional Hurst cars were painted from 1969–1973 (Pontiacs and Oldsmobiles included).

The convertible 300-H has hand-applied pinstriping, and the stripe color, pattern, and design are different from the 300-H hardtops. George wanted this car to be special. In addition, the lower body was painted Hurst Gold for a more dramatic effect. Mr. Hurst wanted his car to be different and stand out from the standard production 300 Hursts, as he was the primary pilot in 1970.

In addition to the paint, the body had a few slight differences from the hardtop Hursts. The rear quarter-panel extension cap seams were filled for a more integrated and cleaner look. The "300-H/Hurst" emblems are in different locations from the production hardtops.

The convertible has the 300-H emblems located on the front fenders above the side-marker lights and one in the center of the decklid lip that faces the rear. Also, there is no Chrysler lettering on the decklid like the standard production 300-H hardtops have, and there are no Chrysler emblems on the car.

Some things must be done correctly or not done at all, and the 300-H convertible does have a factory-installed Hurst shifter. There is no way that George Hurst was going to drive this car without having his shifter in place.

An interesting fact is the Hurst Auto-Stick shifter is designed to only work with column-shift linkage. This is why this car was specifically ordered with a column shift from Chrysler and then converted by Hurst to an Auto-Stick. This wasn't an afterthought. The car was intended to have this shifter from Day 1.

300-H at the Track

The 300-H convertible was a common site at racetracks in the East, Midwest, South, West Coast, and Canada from mid-1970 through 1972. Usually, Miss Hurst Golden Shifter Linda Vaughn

Parade duties were a specialty for the Chrysler 300-H. Here, Miss Hurst Golden Shifter Linda Vaughn bows for fans as a pair of lucky attendants get to ride in the back of the car. (Photo Courtesy Fred Von Sholly)

Shifting is, in a way, how current owner Trev Dellinger came to be the new caretaker of Mopar history.

"I was just very, very fortunate, and I happened to be the right guy for the car, I guess," Dellinger said.

Dellinger has been a C-Body Mopar guy from almost Day 1.

"I've always liked big cars and purpose-built vehicles," he said.

Dellinger has a humble-yet-unique collection of some pretty rare fuselage-era Chrysler vehicles.

"Purpose-built cars are appealing to me," he said. "Police cars, race cars, taxis, high-performance cars, etc. were built for a specific reason, and the 300-Hurst convertible fits that category perfectly. The car was built specifically as a Hurst/Chrysler promotional vehicle, and it has an amazing history. This car was at every major drag race from 1970 to 1972, and it's pretty bad ass."

Dellinger told the story of how he became the caretaker of the convertible.

"The car was really unknown by the car community," he said. "Only some Chrysler 300 Club members knew about it. It was in noted Chrysler collector Steve McCloud's collection for years, and he didn't bring it out often.

"When I was in high school, circa 1986, a local Chrysler Hurst collector in the Seattle area, Jim Harris, showed me a photo in a book of the Hurst convertible. He said, 'Kid, that's *the* car. That's the one you want.'

"I never forgot what Jim said that day. The fact that I have it now is really special—a dream come true, really. I have to pinch myself every time I look at it to remind myself that it's really mine."

However, he didn't do it alone. Dellinger's friend Bill Hanzlik, also known as "Billy Fury," a noted Chrysler collector of rare C-Body cars, was instrumental in convincing Dellinger to purchase the car. After many discussions with Hanzlik about the Hurst convertible and its history, Hanzlik said, "Trev, just do it. Get the car."

It was good advice.

The First Public Owner

Dellinger told the McCloud family that his intention was to show the car to the car world and Mopar community and not park it in a museum.

"I took the car to the Chrysler Nationals at Carlisle in 2016, and the unthinkable happened," Dellinger said.

He met the first public owner, who was unknown until that time.

"A gentleman named Ted Dillard walked up to me,"

After George Hurst, Ted Dillard was the next owner of the 1970 Chrysler 300-H. Here, the car sits outside his residence in September 1973. (Photo Courtesy Ted Dillard)

Dellinger said. "He asked if I owned the car, and I said that I did. He looked at the car, specifically the interior, and said, 'I bought this car from Jack Duffy, the vice president of Hurst Performance Research, in September 1973.'"

Dellinger was stunned.

"That was truly amazing," Dellinger said. "Ted Dillard was the missing link in the history of the car."

Dillard was a Mopar guy and had owned many muscle cars, including Hemi 'Cudas and Chargers. Dillard met Jack Duffy at a drag race and asked what Hurst was going to do with the car.

"We will probably sell it soon," Duffy said.

"I'd like to buy it," Dillard replied.

In September 1973, Dillard did just that. He took photos when he took delivery of the convertible at Duffy's house, and he

Current owner Trev Dellinger (left) shakes the hand of Ted Dillard (right) at the 2016 Chrysler Nationals. This was the first ever meeting between the two, and it was unplanned. (Photo Courtesy Trev Dellinger)

An Owner's Perspective

also wrote to Hurst and asked about the history of the 300-H convertible. Jack Duffy and Dick Chrysler from Hurst Performance were kind enough to write back to Dillard and list part numbers, paint codes, and production numbers for all the Chrysler Hurst cars. The best part is that Dillard kept the letters from Hurst, Duffy, and Dick Chrysler and gave them to Dellinger to go with the car. Now the complete ownership history is known.

"I couldn't believe it when Mr. Dillard told me that he bought the car from Hurst, and he said, 'I think I have some letters from Hurst about the car,'" Dellinger said. "That was simply amazing for the car and its history.

"For me it's about preserving Mopar and drag-racing history and showing the collector car and Mopar community this flawed diamond and these unique Chrysler 300 Hursts."

That's what it's all about.

and the Hurstettes (Nikki Phillips, June Cochran, and Marsha Bennett) were riding on the back with either Linda or Nikki on platform duty, which meant riding on the platform with a giant 12-foot Hurst shifter.

George Hurst drove the convertible 300-H quite often. Linda Vaughn told me the following story at MCACN in 2016. I was talking to Linda about the convertible 300-H, and I kept calling it her car. She interrupted and said, "Honey, this isn't my car. This was George's car. It was his favorite car of all the cars we had, and he drove it as much as he could any time that he could."

So, the 1970 300-H convertible is George's car. Perfect.

1971 FORD MUSTANG BOSS 302

By Wes Eisenschenk

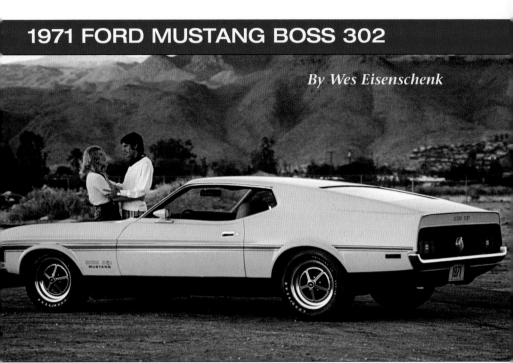

This publicity photo by Ford Motor Company shows the Boss 302 wearing 351 decals. Ford used prototypes and mules for multiple purposes, and most wore many hats. (Photo Courtesy Ford Motor Company)

There are countless stories in the history of the muscle car where a particular model ended up on the cutting-room floor. In these pages you will read about the 1972 440-6 Chargers and Road Runners that were slated for production only to be killed off after a few early copies escaped the crusher. Another similar pair of cars on these pages are the 1967 Shelby GT500 convertible and the 1983 Corvette.

There are a host of reasons why a car is given a hard look at production only to end up being yanked from the option list at the last minute. Most of these cars are classified as being one of the following:

- preproduction
- prototype
- pilot order
- pilot job
- test mule
- engineering test car
- publicity vehicle
- introductory show unit

The workload for these vehicles vary. For example, I owned 9F02R100031. This car was initially created to be an introductory show unit. Its purpose was to go to a region in North America where it might end up at an early-year model show or be used for press purposes. However, my old car was plucked from the inventory of show units and procured by Kar-Kraft for Boss 429 wheel and tire development. It's technically KK1201, the first Boss 429 Mustang.

As a test mule, it wore more hats at Ford. At one point it was sent to Paul Shedlik. Paul was a fabricator used by Ford Motor Company and an expert in fiberglass work. KK1201 was used by Shedlik to create a mold for "Ohio" George Montgomery's 1969 Mach 1 drag racing gasser. There's no telling what other mule work that the car was used for at Ford. Eventually, it found its way to Ford's resale lot and was authorized to be sold on May 6, 1969.

The next car I discuss checks the box on several of those above-listed classifications.

Boss 302

After back-to-back years (1969 and 1970) of producing successful production homologation models for its Mustang Trans-Am racing enterprise, Ford Motor Company explored adding the Boss 302 engine to its new bodystyle for 1971. The "Boss" nickname had been applied to two Mustangs in those prior years using its engine displacement as the model's name (302 and 429). It's thought that Ford wanted to duplicate that endeavor again for 1971 with Boss 302- and 351-powered Mustangs.

As Ford ramped up tooling and for its dual-Boss efforts, a series of events likely altered Ford's decision in moving forward with two Boss Mustangs. First, a Sports Car Club of America (SCCA) rule change allowed for bigger motors to be used. The second was that Ford was getting ready to pull the plug on producing race cars and sponsoring sanctioned racing in the United States.

1971 Boss 302

Research indicates that a total of seven 1971 Boss 302s were scheduled to be built at the Metuchen, New Jersey, plant for various work prior to the model-year production run. Of those seven cars, just three were "bucked," which means that the shells were created.

There initially were two 1971 Boss 302 prototypes: the yellow market-ing car and this blue Mustang. This car was used for testing at one of Ford's proving grounds. (Photo Courtesy Ford Motor Company)

It's alleged that they were destroyed once the program was canceled. However, the Dearborn, Michigan, assembly plant was likely ahead on its program and yielded the creation of only two 1971 Boss 302s.

The Medium Blue Metallic Boss

In the October 1970 issue of *Super Stock and Drag Illustrated*, a Medium Blue Metallic 1971 Boss 302 was featured. This car's rear tail panel, tail shield, and lower doors, fenders, and rockers were painted in Argent. Wheel covers were attached to the steel wheels with Fires-tone Wide Oval rubber. The Boss also featured rear and chin spoil-ers. "BOSS 302" decals were affixed to both front fenders above the Mustang emblem, and the rear decklid had the same script above the trunk lock. Dual mirrors and an Argent hockey stripe capped off the exterior. A Ram Air hood is shown in the publicity shots.

A Ford engineer recalled driving this car at the Ford test track and thought it may not have survived because it lacked certain safety equipment.

The Grabber Yellow Boss

Our feature Boss was built at the Dearborn assembly plant on August 3, 1970. This Boss 302's first item of business was a fall display at the Las Vegas Convention Center in the new car display for Ford Motor Company. The gate release invoice was dated August 4, 1970. Typically, new cars hit the showrooms in early September, giving you an idea of the compacted schedule between them heading for mass production and the termination of the Boss 302 option.

It's unclear if the Mustang wore its 302 attire at the show or if it was converted to wear the Boss 351 decals. What *is* clear is that the promotional photo of the car featured at the beginning of the story shows a mountainous backdrop in what appears to be a valley. This could easily have been staged before or after the convention display, although

The contrasting red interior resonates strongly against the yellow paint. In the background, the other marketing cars await their turn for a publicity shot. (Photo Courtesy Ford Motor Company)

that's speculation until the backdrop for the car can be confirmed.

In the promotional photo, the rear deck and fender 351-decal lettering have been crudely changed with the "5" and "1" looking as though they've been superimposed over the removed "0" and "2."

Evolution

The Grabber Yellow Boss began its hat dance either before or after the Las Vegas Convention Center display. As noted earlier, the decals and lettering were swapped out for 351 lettering during the promotional shoot. With the change to 351 attire came a change to the door tag and VIN, as the car became 1F02R100053 on an invoice dated December 23, 1970. Former owner Andrew Hack summed up the transformation in my previous book *Lost Muscle Cars*.

"It should be noted for those unfamiliar with the Mustang VINs and bodystyles that a standard fastback or SportsRoof Mustang bodystyle is an '02' body code, hence the '1F02' preface in the VIN. The Mach 1 bodystyle is the same fastback body but has Mach 1 trim added and an '05' in the VIN, hence the '1F05' preface in the VIN. The Boss 302 cars, not being Mach 1s, were designated as '02' SportsRoofs and carried a 'G' code for the Boss 302 motor in the VIN, hence '1F02G.' The later-released Boss 351 cars used an 'R' motor code, hence the '1F02R' in the VIN. Since no Mustang could be both a Mach 1 and a Boss, there could be no '1F05R' or '1F05G' VIN, as both 'G' and 'R' motor codes were reserved for Boss-only builds."

What all of this means is that the 1F02 Boss 302 changed to become a 1F05R Mach 1 with Boss 351 decals. However, there was no such thing as a 1F05R Boss, as the 1971 variants started with VIN 1F02R. No Mach 1s ever had the R engine, so Ford inadvertently created another 1 of 1. But wait, there's more!

On February 25, 1971, the Mustang received its final designation as VIN 1F02H100053, a 1971 SportsRoof with a 351 2-barrel carburetor. The car was sent to Wilson Ford in Huntington Beach, California, for resale.

Take a minute and grab some ibuprofen out of your cabinet.

The car was officially all of the following:

- 1 of 2 1971 Boss 302s produced and the only known surviving car
- The only Mach 1 R-code ever built
- The first 1971 Boss 351
- The only 351 2-barrel 4-speed Toploader car ever built

After over a decade of owning the car, Andrew got together with Bob Perkins, a noted Mustang restorer and collector in Wisconsin just an hour down the road. Bob had amassed a large collection of 1971 Boss 302 parts over the years but had no car to put them in. Andrew, with the only surviving 1971 Boss 302, and Bob, with all the parts, agreed that one of them should have both the parts and car. A deal was struck, and Bob purchased the rare Mustang.

Restoration

With a motherload of 1971 Boss 302 new old stock (NOS) parts in hand, Bob decided that it was time for the Boss to regain its identity. A concourse restoration began in 2020 to return the Mustang back to its original configuration.

If you were at the Las Vegas Convention Center in the fall of 1970 and photographed this Boss, please give Bob a call. You may have the only surviving photo of the fabled 1971 Boss 302 Mustang.

The missing blue 1971 Boss 302 remains elusive, and some surmise that it may have been crushed. Although, if the yellow car wore many hats, it's probable that the blue car may have as well. (Photo Courtesy Ford Motor Company)

1971 AMC AMX PROTOTYPE

By Thomas Benvie

The 1971 AMX prototype's side pipes, red striping, and blue paint against a red interior create a striking color combination. (Photo Courtesy Mike Spangler)

The AMC AMX concept started just prior to 1964. Richard "Dick" Teague joined the American Motors design team in 1959, which was headed by Edmund Anderson. By 1961, Teague was appointed the principal designer when Anderson left the company. Teague's influence can be found in the Rambler Classic and the Ambassador—the first all-new cars from American Motors since 1956. However, it was some behind-the-scenes work that got more of Teague's attention.

Tarpon

Using the newly engineered platform from a 1964 Rambler American, Teague designed an all-new 2+2 seating configuration that was called the Tarpon. He envisioned an all-new segment of the industry, which later became known as the pony car category with the introduction of the Ford Mustang.

Teague loved to repurpose old designs into new cars, and when he saw the fastback 1963 Corvettes, he thought of the prewar fastback cars and was inspired. First shown at the private Society of Automotive Engineers (SAE) convention in January 1964, the car was on stage with some AMC designers who were working on a cutaway version. The concept was very well received.

Its official debut was at the 1964 Chicago Auto Show. The bright red with black roof design study was an immediate hit. At the 1964 New York International Auto Show, it was displayed near the Mustang II concept design and received equal approval from the masses. More than 60 percent of those surveyed stated they would buy one, and remember, this was only a four-passenger vehicle, so it was not for everyone. Alas, it did not go into production.

AMC was still in the middle of developing its second-generation lightweight V-8 engine that could fit in the small Rambler American chassis. It later became the 290-ci engine and the basis for all V-8s up to the 401-ci engine.

Furthermore, AMC's CEO Roy Abernathy wanted to move away from the image that AMC only made small cars, and he led the company into the more-profitable larger-size cars. People thought that AMC Rambler only made plain cars, and Abernathy wished to change that public perception. Although the car eventually grew to the larger 3+3 Marlin, the proportions and image had changed.

Project IV

Not one to be dissuaded, Teague went to work on a new set of 1966 concept cars called Project IV. These four cars were exercises engineered around the American platform and were used to promote some of the features in upcoming cars. It also helped gauge the public's interest in specifics of the design features.

"While these car concepts are not being shown as actual prototypes, we expect reactions to the innovations presented will have substantial bearing on future design and engineering decisions," Abernathy said. "The cars were first shown in New York, then moved to Washington, D.C., Los Angeles, San Francisco, Chicago, and Detroit.

Cavalier
The Cavalier resurrected a potential design element where body panels on one side of the car interchanged with those on the other so

that the front left fender was the same as the right rear. The hood and decklid and front and rear bumpers were also interchangeable. It was thought this could save 25 percent in the costs of body tooling. The front half design of this car mimics what became the Hornet, which was introduced as a 1970 model.

Vixen

The Vixen was a two-door version of the Cavalier, and thus resembled the soon-to-be-created Hornet. By changing some design elements, such as the grille, it looked like a different vehicle. This concept was later used in the 1968 Javelin/AMX and the 1970 Hornet/Gremlin.

AMX

The biggest hit of the group was the AMX, or American Motors eXperimental. Contrary to belief, the car was not just a two-seater. There was a unique ramble seat that was reminiscent of the old rumble seats, where the trunk opened up into seating. For this car, the rear window opened upward to provide a windscreen. However, if the ramble seat was not open, there was still a contoured rear seat in the back, which may have been for looks only. This car was Teague's passion, and he was determined to make it work.

AMX II

The fourth car was the AMX II. Although it did not actually resemble the AMX on the outside, it was a study of exchanging some exterior panels to make a new car.

1 for 4

Teague received the green light to advance the AMX concept to the next level. Eventually, he succeeded with the introduction of the Javelin in the fall of 1967 as a 1968-model-year car. The Javelin was essentially an AMX with 12 inches added to the center section that accommodated a back seat.

The new second-generation engine debuted in 1966 as a 290-ci version that was available in both 2- and 4-barrel versions. Floor- or column-shift automatics, plus 3- or 4-speed manual transmissions were also available in the Rogue. For 1967, the engine size changed to 343 ci. With the debut of the AMX, the displacement was increased to 390, and the engine was aptly named the AMX 390 in whatever model it was used.

The two-seater AMX debuted to the public on February 15, 1968, at the Daytona International Speedway, just four months after the Javelin was introduced. With straight-line runs of 130-plus mph and some gymkhana courses, it was an immediate hit with the press.

With a different hood skin, grille, and marker lights, it was just enough of a change to make it look like a new model—not to mention the missing 12 inches from the middle and no back seat. This was an ingenious use of common parts to make two separate cars. The new ad agency of Wells, Rich, and Green pushed AMC into performance and set up a record run a month before the car's release.

Into the Record Books

Craig Breedlove and his wife, Lee, set 106 new speed records before the public even saw one of these cars. At a stockholder meeting, it was stated, "We are confident that we will sell over 10,000 AMXs this year."

That prediction was right. Although, only 6,725 AMXs were built in the abbreviated 1968 run, by December 31, there were just over 11,000 1968/1969 two-seaters produced. Since the introduction of the car in February, the Kenosha plant assembled over 300 cars a week in 15 of the 18 weeks to the end of the model year.

When the barely changed 1969 model arrived, once again over 300 cars a week were built from its September introduction to Thanksgiving. There were 6,725 cars produced in the first five months of production, but the expected increase in sales was not realized. Only 4,500 AMXs were made in the first five months of the 1969 model year. The writing was on the wall that the AMX would not be around much longer.

Reskinning the AMX

The design changes for the 1970 model year began almost a year prior to the release. Federal regulations required new taillights and side-marker lights across American Motors' whole car line. Hood scoops were about to become a thing. Boss Mustang, the soon to be released AAR 'Cuda and Challenger T/A, Hemi cars, and Trans Am Firebird all had them. Although it wasn't a scoop, the cowl-induction hood of the Camaro meant that AMC had to change some things if it wanted to be successful. Perhaps one of the smoothest hood scoops was created for the 1970 AMX that was also available on some of the Javelins.

The grille was completely new, and the front bumper was modified, but it looked like a whole new car. The rather plain-looking interior was almost completely new with wood-grain on the dash, new door panel designs, and completely new high-back bucket seats. Once again, it was a freshening that did not cost a lot of money in tooling.

However, it was too little, too late.

In the last 32 weeks of the 1969 model year, barely 150 AMXs were produced each week. For the 1970 year, sales did not improve. There were 19 weeks where fewer than 100 cars were made; 10 of these weeks had fewer than 50. The redesigned Camaro and Firebird, plus the newly released 'Cuda and Challenger and second-year design of the Mustang, were too much for the pony-car field to support. The two-seater AMX did not return for 1971.

One Last Hurrah

Dick Teague was not to be deterred. A newly designed 1971 Javelin was already approved for release. Most of the structure was repurposed from the previous model year but with new outer skins. A whole new interior that used injection-molded plastic, except for the 1970 seats, was also designed. A fiberglass mock-up was used as a proposal to show the American Motors brass. The doors and the cowl were almost identical to the 1968–1970 models.

Teague added the proposed 1971 nose to his personal 1968 AMX. It is believed that the nose was removed from the fiberglass 1971 proposal car. The meeting took place in November 1969, and within a few months, the two-seater AMX was nixed, and the AMX name became a performance upgrade to the Javelin model. Ultimately, Dick Teague created the only AMX to feature both generation styling cues.

Teague's personal AMX was a 1968 390 automatic Go Pak–equipped car that was white with black stripes and a red interior. It was equipped with tilt wheel, AM/8-track, and air conditioning.

At one point, he saw black painted bumpers on the Javelin of coworker Fred Hudson. He liked the look enough that he did the same to his white car. This became a feature of the three Big Bad

Colors along with rear bumper guards. He also changed his stripe to red and added a modified center fold-down armrest, which was only available on 4-speed-equipped cars. A painted modified front spoiler and a Group 19 rear wing spoiler were additions as well as fog lights in the grille and hood pins.

For looks, the AMX quarter-circle emblems were changed to dummy quick-release gas caps. The letters "AMX" were added to the rear of the front fenders, along with the separate numbers 390 to designate the engine size. A set of factory-authorized Sidewinder side exhaust pipes, Goodyear E70x14 raised white-letter tires, and a passenger-door side mirror rounded out the upgrades. Unfortunately, the mirror was mounted incorrectly.

Even though Teague failed at bringing forth the next generation of two-door AMXs to AMC, he succeeded in creating one of the most unusual 1 of 1 muscle cars of all time, and for that we say, "Thank you, Mr. Teague."

The adjustable rear spoiler gives the hybrid AMX a racy look. (Photo Courtesy Mike Spangler)

1971 PONTIAC VENTURA SPRINT 455

By Wes Eisenschenk

Hood tachometer? Check. Honeycomb wheels? Check. 455 H.O. call-outs? Check. The only box that the 1971 Ventura II Sprint didn't check was being produced en masse by Pontiac. (Photo Courtesy Martyn Schorr)

Coulda, woulda, shoulda.

How many times have you read something about a concept car or prototype that makes you smirk and shake your head at the same time? For Pontiac enthusiasts, these last two attempts at performance muscle cars may have been the walk-off shot that would have settled the debate of who was king of the muscle-car era.

Many muscle-car fans cite 1970 as the high-water mark of the muscle-car era. This attribution is mostly placed on that year due to General Motors lifting its under-400-ci-displacement threshold on cars smaller than the full-size models offered by each manufacturer. In prior years, there were avenues to circumvent the ban (central office production order [COPO], Hurst, and super-car builders), but for most new car purchasers, there wasn't anything on the order sheet to combat the 428 Cobra Jet Fords and 440- and 426-powered Pentastars.

That all changed in 1970 when the seven-year ban on 400-ci-and-over displacement was hoisted off the shoulders of GM engine designers. A flood of 454 and 455 engines were made available across the spectrum as the playing field evened out on the street.

No, It's Not a Nova!

As Pontiac bathed in the pool of high-performance 455-equipped Firebirds, Trans Ams, and GTOs, Chevrolet gorged on a segment of the market that Buick, Oldsmobile, and the aforementioned Pontiac brand didn't have in its stable: the compact.

Nova sales on the rebodied Chevy II grew from 163,552 cars in 1968 to 251,849 in 1969. By 1970, an astounding 307,280 units barreled through the assembly lines within the walls of General Motors.

Having been on the sidelines far too long, Pontiac was the first brand within GM to offer a counterpart. It rebranded the Ventura nameplate from the Catalina line and placed it on its new compact, the 1971 Ventura II.

Nova sales dropped for the first time since 1967, as 194,878 units passed through the gates. The upstart Ventura II snagged 48,484 sales from customers who finally had an option other than the bowtie compact.

I Call and Raise

Chevrolet had abandoned its big-block Nova after 1970 and settled on a pair of 350-optioned engines (245 and 270 hp) as the lone performance displacement offerings for 1971. The Ventura II's largest-displacement engine for 1971 was the 307 2-barrel that had a modest 200 hp.

However, Pontiac had big plans for 1972.

1971 Pontiac Ventura II Sprint 455

Whether it was attempting to fill a hole in the marketplace or create a buzz that might set off alarms, Pontiac unveiled a 1971 Ventura II Sprint 455 for the press at the model preview display held at GM's Milford Proving Ground in the summer of 1971.

Royal Automotive's Milt Schornack was tasked with preparing a Ventura II Sprint for the magazine scribes to ring out. A Bronze metallic 1971 Ventura II Sprint was selected as the donor car for the build. The Sprint's decal package consisted of a long side stripe in gold metallic paint. The Poncho featured power steering, power brakes, front and rear sway bars, bucket seats, a console with a floor shifter, and an AM radio. The car rode on honeycomb wheels with F60-14

The F60-15 Goodyear Polyglas GTs were the tire of choice for the prototype. (Photo Courtesy Martyn Schorr)

It doesn't look like much, but a 455 H.O. lurks beneath this air cleaner. I'm sure the power brakes were much needed to slow the front-heavy Ventura II down. (Photo Courtesy Martyn Schorr)

Polyglas tires bolted on all four corners. The first order of business was the removal of the 307 Chevrolet mill and its Powerglide transmission.

The stock motor mounts were removed and replaced with a set of Firebird 455 candle holders. A 455 mated to a Turbo Hydra-Matic transmission was installed and paired with the deepest rear gearset for a Nova: a 3.42 Positraction rear end. A hood-mounted tachometer tied it all together.

To compensate for the extra weight on the nose, heavy-duty coil springs from a Firebird were supplemented in the front for the stock units.

Just two accounts of the car made it to print. Martyn Schorr of *Hi-Performance Cars* magazine and Jim McCraw with *Super Stock & Drag Illustrated* each spent some time behind the wheel in 1971. While Schorr noted that his time with the car was in June, the *Super Stock & Drag Illustrated* feature may have been earlier, as there were no leaves on the trees in the photos.

Schorr recalled in his book *Day One: An Automotive Journalist's Muscle-Car Memoir* that the Ventura II cornered "extremely flat and was easily controllable at high speeds through the cones."

A full feature on the car was showcased in *Super Stock & Drag Illustrated*. McCraw noted that Schornack met him at the Detroit airport and they had an all-day affair with the car. McCraw also noted that "in tight turns, body roll was almost absent," as a 45-minute commute to Milan Dragway yielded opportunities to test the car on on-ramps and off-ramps and on butterfly acceleration and handling tests.

Acceleration Tests

Safely in the confines of Milan Dragway, Schornack and McCraw agreed that the only modifications needed on the car were timing and jetting. The group made a total of 13 passes down the track and dropped initial ETs from a modest 14.85 at 99.4 mph and finished with a 13.98 at 101.12. The F60s and 3.42 rear held back the car's true potential. Still, it was a 100-mph quarter-mile car that choked and puked through a single exhaust.

Super Car Ventura?

The Pontiac Ventura II was too late to the game. Pontiac was late to respond to the Nova and offer a competitive engine package for

Chevy's 350. Just like borrowing something from someone you detest, Pontiac had to borrow Chevy's X-Body platform and its engine packages. The 455 Ventura II may have restored some of that dignity and given the Chevy Novas a punch in the mouth on the street. However, it was all for naught. This lone factory-supported super car was Pontiac's only volley, or it was perhaps a flailing flare at best.

Pontiac's 455 H.O. found its way into the full-size and midsize lineups. This lone Ventura II may be the only X-Body-platform-based, factory-supported car ever to receive a big-block in 1971. (Photo Courtesy Martyn Schorr)

1983 CHEVROLET CORVETTE

By Scott Kolecki

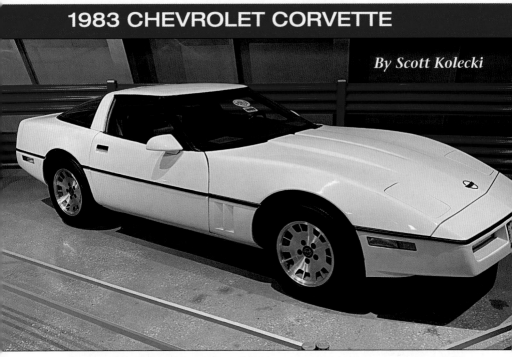

Nearly 60 1983 Corvette test mules and pilot cars were created. This car avoided being destroyed, perhaps because it was at GM's Milford proving grounds for testing. (Photo Courtesy Scott Kolecki)

Since its creation nearly 40 years ago, there has always been a mystique surrounding the existence (or lack thereof) of the 1983 Corvette. There are naysayers and conspiracy theorists within the Corvette community who claim Chevrolet elected to skip the 1983 model year entirely. The most common explanations offered over the years have ranged from re-tooling issues at GM's new Bowling Green assembly plant that prevented the on-time start of production to design to a variety of technology issues with the car itself. While there are elements of truth to both these reasons, the actual answer is a bit more complicated.

A Brief History

The evolution of the fourth-generation Corvette began in 1979 under the direction of David McLellan, Corvette's chief engineer, and Jerry Palmer, the chief designer of the Chevrolet III Studio. Although the car's outward aesthetic, aerodynamic profile, and preliminary mechanical underpinnings took the better part of a year to develop, a viable prototype was presented to Chevrolet's product policy group (PPG) on April 22, 1980. The PPG was so impressed with the next-generation Corvette that it immediately approved the design for production.

The next-generation Corvette continued to be refined into a viable production-model prototype over the next two years. Benefitting from a plethora of additional engineering resources that had been specifically assigned to its development as part of a robust prototype program, the latest Corvette evolved quickly. It was even thought, at least briefly, that the new Corvette would replace the third-generation model beginning in 1982.

Ongoing difficulties with several of its engineering and technology packages prevented the car from being ready as a 1982 production model. Instead, GM scheduled the fourth-generation Corvette's press reveal for the fall of 1982 at Riverside International Raceway. Even as its official debut edged ever closer, several questions remained unanswered by GM, including how much the new Corvette would cost, when Chevrolet officially planned to begin production, and, most importantly, would it be a 1983 or 1984 model-year car?

Common conjecture was that Chevrolet planned to release the latest Corvette as a 1983 model, but that decision changed after the federal government introduced new legislation that required stricter

Before prototypes, there were clay models. Each side of the clay model was often developed in a contrasting design so that the brass could compare one versus the other. (Photo Courtesy General Motors)

exhaust and emissions standards. Testing of the next-generation Corvette's exhaust and emissions systems was already underway when the new federal requirements were published. It was decided that GM's engineering group should be afforded the extra time needed to ensure that the car met the updated requirements, which also meant it would skip a year of commercial production.

The Corvette program benefitted from skipping the 1983 model year in several ways. First, it meant that the new Corvette was built to meet 1984 federal emissions certification standards, provided that production began on or after January 1, 1983. Second, it meant that the car only had to complete one federal certification process, which provided a sizable cost savings to General Motors. Third, and perhaps most importantly, it gave Corvette's engineers added time to focus on getting it right over simply getting it done.

Even after the decision was made to postpone commercial production until 1984, Chevrolet elected to manufacture 14 test mules and 43 pilot cars with unique 1983 VINs. Most of these cars were produced to allow GM engineers and designers the opportunity to field test (and in so doing, further refine) the new Corvette's performance and handling capabilities, while the remainder of the cars were showcased at press events and marketing forums to evaluate consumer opinion of the fourth-generation model.

The lone 1983 Corvette resides in the National Corvette Museum in Bowling Green, Kentucky. Luckily, it survived the sinkhole collapse of February 12, 2014. (Photo Courtesy Scott Kolecki)

Form Versus Function

The 1983 Corvettes marked the first time in the brand's history that virtually every major assembly of the car represented how form follows function. It featured a drag coefficient (Cd) of 0.341 to make it the lowest coefficient to date. This was achieved through extensive wind-tunnel testing during the car's development. Every surface was subjected to rigorous aerodynamic analysis to maximize the car's slipperiness at any speed.

A significant part of its impressive aerodynamic envelope was directly attributed to its acute windshield rake of 64.7 degrees. Between that, a pair of uniquely concealed headlamps that rotated backward to prevent drag, aerodynamically shaped side mirrors, minimal bodyside rub strips, and a frameless rear glass window that doubled as a hatch assembly, the 1983 Corvette had virtually nothing that could create drag or wind buffeting, even when operating at high speeds.

Even with its single-piece roof panel removed (the previous generation had a center bar/T-top configuration), the vehicle's occupants could enjoy an open-air experience without encountering a barrage of turbulent air inside the cockpit.

Throughout the engineering process, there was a continual underlying objective to advance the car's directional stability, on-center steering, and ability to corner. This resulted in the evolution of an all-new, lightweight uni-frame assembly that was strong and "highly resistant to the strenuous flex that can reduce tire-patch contact with road surfaces during cornering," according to the National Corvette Museum.

The car received a reimagined suspension system. The front coilover springs were replaced with a single, fiberglass composite mono-leaf transverse spring. Unequal-length control arms and steering knuckles made of forged aluminum were introduced as a weight-saving measure as well as for their extreme tensile strength. The rear suspension was also fitted with a transverse, fiberglass composite mono-leaf spring. This was paired to a five-link independent system that was comprised of forged aluminum knuckles that were located fore and aft by aluminum upper and lower trailing links and laterally via strut and tie-rod assemblies.

The Heartbeat of the 1983 Corvette

One of the most significant enhancements made to the 1983 Corvette (and the fourth-generation model as a whole) was the introduction of a front shroud in lieu of a conventional hood. Where previous Corvettes had a forward-opening hood assembly, the 1983 Corvette utilized a single-piece clamshell-style front shroud that allowed unobstructed access to the car's engine and front suspension.

Chevrolet introduced a 5.7L, 350-ci V-8 engine as the sole powerplant for the 1983 Corvette. The engine featured a twin throttle body with Cross-Fire fuel injection. Although it was originally introduced in the 1982 Corvette, this new L83 engine was considered by many to be one of the best high-performance engines of its day and a perfect powerplant for the technologically advanced fourth-generation model.

The L83 engine was paired to a 4-speed automatic transmission with overdrive, although GM had also planned to offer the optional, all-new Doug Nash 4+3 manual transmission that provided consumers a 4-speed gearbox with automatic overdrive for its top three gears. This no-cost option was offered to consumers beginning in 1984. A rear axle with a gear ratio of 3.31:1 made up the car's rear end. The 1983 Corvette's powertrain propelled the car from 0 to 60 in less than 7 seconds and delivered a top speed of 140 mph.

Chevrolet engineers partnered with Goodyear for the 1983 and subsequent fourth-generation Corvettes to create a purpose-built tire for its new sports car. Goodyear utilized much of its existing Formula 1 rain-tire technology to develop a new performance tire that was perfectly suited for the new Corvette. The result was a set of 15-inch Eagle VR tires with natural path treads perfectly engineered to handle everything that the 1983 Corvettes threw at them. These direction-specific tires were a beefy P215/65R15. Interestingly, a 16-inch version of these tires was introduced for the 1984 model year.

To complement the car's agile cornering and robust acceleration, the 1983 Corvette was fitted with a Gridlock four-wheel disc-brake system. Known for its proven high-performance-racing braking capabilities, Gridlock's low-drag, aluminum caliper design provided the new Corvette with exceptional braking power.

The 1983 Corvette had a curb weight (with a full tank of gas) of 3,192 pounds, which was a marked improvement over the outgoing 1982 model at a weight of 3,342 pounds. It also sat lower (46.7 inches versus 48.4 inches) and wider (71 inches versus 69 inches), and it was nearly 10 inches shorter than the outgoing model (176.5 inches versus 185.3 inches).

The One and Only

While it has been previously established that there were nearly 60 1983 Corvette test mules and pilot cars built at the Bowling Green Corvette assembly plant, only one exists today. That car, VIN 1G1AY0783D5110023, resides at the National Corvette Museum across the street from the Corvette plant. When it was first produced, this car was sent to GM's Milford Proving Ground for an additional shakedown and testing. Like its 42 pilot car counterparts, it was scheduled to be returned to Bowling Green upon the completion of the testing, where it would be destroyed.

What makes the 1983 Corvette such an incredibly rare and special car is that it technically should not exist today. Its survival and continued existence is as much a part of its lore as the car itself. There are a variety of stories that range from frustrated plant employees who concealed the pilot car when they learned that the 1983 Corvette, which would have commemorated the 30th anniversary of the brand, was not going to be produced, to a facilities engineer who left early from his car-crushing duties when a violent thunderstorm threatened to leave him and his new pair of cowboy boots literally caught out in the rain.

No matter how it happened, the one and only 1983 Corvette became a long-term fixture at the Bowling Green assembly plant after Paul Schnoes, the plant's former general manager, discovered the car hidden on the plant's back parking lot. Employees at the plant gave the car a unique stars and stripes paintjob and a pair of 16-inch wheels from the 1984-model-year production line. It spent the next decade on display in the plant's main entrance as a mascot of sorts for the plant's hundreds of employees.

The one and only 1983 Corvette was donated to the National Corvette Museum to celebrate its grand opening on September 2, 1994. The car's exterior was returned to its original white paint color, and the original 15-inch wheels were reinstalled. The car continues to be a highlight of the museum's collection to this day.

While some consider the 1983 Corvette to be a successful failure in that it never advanced to production despite the sizable efforts of so many people assigned to its creation, a great many more look at the 1983 Corvette as an outward example of General Motors' intent to keep its focus on getting it right over simply getting it done.

CHAPTER 2

Factory Production Cars

We've all been to the car show where someone declares on a display board that their car is 1 of 1. Likely, they're correct. Nearly every car can fall into this category based on options, and some even go so far as to denote the day that the car was built as applicable criteria. Well, that's just nonsense.

A true 1 of 1 must come down to unique drivetrain components or be the only one ever built in a specific color. There are a handful of options that move the value needle as well. Of course, not all manufacturers have records on paint, so we have to go with what currently exists or was recorded to have existed.

When it comes down to it, a 1 of 1 car is more valuable than its mass-produced counterpart.

With this criteria, we can ascertain what is a book-worthy addition as opposed to what ends up on the cutting-room floor. Pitchforks be damned.

1965 CHEVROLET CHEVELLE 300 COPO 9719

By Wes Eisenschenk

The 300 Deluxe model made for quite a difference aesthetically from its more-flashy Super Sport model. Gone was the hood chrome strip, wheel well molding, and special grill. (Photo Courtesy Mike Smith)

Semon "Bunkie" Knudsen has an American automotive success story unlike anyone before or since. Bred into the car business, Bunkie's father, William "Big Bill" Knudsen, rose through the ranks at Ford Motor Company after he started in 1911. He left for Chevrolet in 1921 and became president of the Chevrolet division of General Motors from 1924 to 1937. He finally ascended to president of General Motors from 1937 to 1940. Having watched his father achieve the highest of positions in automobile manufacturing, it can be assumed that anything less than that for Bunkie was a failure. Fortunately for Bunkie, he surpassed his father's career in more ways than one.

With an engineering degree in hand, Bunkie entered GM in the tool-making department in 1939. Bunkie's meteoric rise through the ranks paralleled his father's. He first became an assembly superintendent for Pontiac and then was a chief inspector within the division. After successfully switching over to be a production manager during World War II and outproducing the other manufacturers in creating weapons (GM received the Battle Efficiency "E" award, which was the first such award ever issued to an auto manufacturer), Knudsen rapidly ascended to general manager of Detroit Diesel in 1955.

He followed that with the position of general manager of the Pontiac division in 1956. Knudsen's Wide Track program at Pontiac in 1959 is often seen as the beginning point of the sales boom and image change for the brand because it offered sporty, performance-oriented affordable vehicles for GM. Knudsen's success in turning the flailing old man's car into the new gotta-have-it machine foreshadowed his greatest contribution to the automotive world: the muscle car.

Pontiac Performance

Pontiac's reputation grew at the strip thanks in part to the wheelmen, such as Arnie "the Farmer" Beswick, Hayden Proffitt (a driver for Mickey Thompson), and Jim Wangers. However, they weren't the only ones seizing the opportunity to use Pontiac's newest big-block: the 421. "Fast" Eddie Kanter, who worked for the Pontiac Motor Division of Detroit, was one of many who capitalized on Bunkie's vision of seeing the brand lead the way into the muscle-car era.

Eddie's loyalty to Bunkie and Pontiac took hold in the late 1950s when he raced Pontiacs at Detroit Dragway. Eddie received go-fast parts from Pontiac's endless supply of performance hardware, and Bunkie reaped the rewards of having his brand in victory lane. It was a formula carved out by most of the manufacturers as their factory drivers boosted the image of their brands. However, when Bunkie became general manager of Chevrolet in November 1961, Eddie stuck with his poncho power at the track, but it wasn't a permanent arrangement.

Chevrolet Performance

With the success of the Wide Track under his belt, Bunkie looked to create something similar to boost Chevrolet's image as well. Enter the 1961 Impala Super Sport. With a new engine (409) and a cleaned-up platform, the Impala Super Sport was the car that thrust Chevrolet back into the performance marketplace. Once the ball started rolling, the Super Sport package was applied to the Nova (1963) and Chevelle/ El Camino (1964) as Chevrolet included this option across its three best-selling genres: full-size, midsize, and compact.

Chevelle SS

Chevrolet had something that could compete cosmetically with cross-town rival Pontiac, but in 1964, the GTO still had 62 cubic inches on its foe. Knudsen's vacancy at Pontiac was filled by protégé Elliott M. "Pete" Estes as John DeLorean filled Pete's vacant job as Pontiac's chief engineer.

Bunkie Knudsen finally pulled even with Pontiac in 1965. The all-new hot one was the Chevelle Malibu SS 396 (Z16), which had 375 hp and was offered at the tail end of the model year in June 1965. Chevrolet finally had its GTO counterpart, but our friend Eddie Kanter had something better up his sleeve.

COPO 9719

Whether or not Eddie had a personal relationship with Bunkie Knudsen is unknown. What is known is that he was somehow able to pull the strings that created the most unique Chevelle ever.

In June 1965, Eddie placed an order through Floyd Foren Chevrolet Inc. in Ferndale, Michigan, for a 1965 Chevelle 300. As mundane as that sounds, the car he ordered was anything but that. Utilizing the COPO program that was typically used for fleet ordering, Eddie created the ultimate Chevelle. In what can only be thought of as ordering off of an à la carte menu, Eddie loaded and unloaded his 300 with the intention to develop the lightest and fastest Chevelle ever imagined.

The first item selected was the Corvette's 425-hp L78 396 Turbo Jet engine with a transistorized ignition and solid lifters. This was the only 1965 Chevelle to ever receive this motor. The fabled M22 Rock Crusher 4-speed was mated to the powerplant and transferred the power back to an unreal set of 4.88 Positraction gears. As an apples-to-apples comparison, the Z16 came stock with the 375-hp L37 Turbo Jet engine, hydraulic lifters, and a 3.31 open rear end. The goodies didn't stop there.

The COPO received the convertible's boxed frame for rigidity and heavier sway bars to handle the increased torque. Larger 11-inch drum brakes were bolted on to help slow the Chevelle at the end of the traps. The 300 models were 200 pounds lighter than their hardtop cousins, and the car came without a radio, exterior mirrors, rocker molding, or carpeting. It wore 7.74x14 gold-line tires with mag-style wheel covers. There was no power steering or brakes, but oddly it came with a heater.

By all accounts, Eddie used the car as a street terror on Woodward Avenue and made the occasional pass at the drag strip, although no official time slips remain.

New Caretaker

As Eddie neared retirement at GM in the late 1960s, he and his wife, Dimple, decided to move their family south to Cookeville, Tennessee. Eddie set up a speed shop in Cookeville, and it was there where Mike Smith (the current owner and Dimple's cousin) encountered the car. As Eddie's life began to turn from the Chevelle, he began the process of selling and trading off some of the go-fast components of the 300. The engine and rear were traded for a wrecked 1966 Cutlass. The interior of the Cutlass replaced the stock interior of the 300. Eddie set up the front bench seat of the Chevelle in his office for customers to sit on.

It's cars like this that fly under the radar for so long. This unassuming 1965 Chevelle is the very definition of hiding in plain sight. (Photo Courtesy Mike Smith)

With 17-year-old Mike in need of transportation, Eddie struck him a deal, and he became the second owner of the COPO for the lofty sum of $1,200. Mike didn't know anything about the history of the car. He was just eager to have his own ride. In a Nostradamus-like fashion, Eddie told Mike to hold onto the original window sticker. The window sticker denoted code 9719A Special Chassis Equipment with the bolstered price of $1,474 added onto the $2,264 base price of the 300.

Authentication

Mike had always known how special his car was thanks to Eddie. We've all been at a car show when someone tells you about their 440 Hemi Mopar that was special ordered from the factory. Most of the

This lone 300 Deluxe joined the 1965 Corvette and Impala L78 cars as the only Chevrolets produced in 1965 that sported 425 hp under the hood. (Photo Courtesy Mike Smith)

time, it's met with a curious look and some playful acknowledgment of what they're saying.

Mike was at work one day when he passed Bob Vance's office. He noticed a photo of a 1966 Chevelle 300 Deluxe on the wall and struck up a conversation about his 1965. Bob played along as Mike told him about 4.88 gears, a Rock Crusher transmission, and a Corvette engine from the factory in his 300.

A couple of weeks later, Bob was thumbing through the latest edition of the National Chevelle Owners Association magazine. Chevelle expert Mark Meekins offered production numbers on the Z16s. In passing, he commented about the quantity built (201) and a single

The 300 Deluxe carried no warning out back about what was going on up front. (Photo Courtesy Mike Smith)

order for an oddball 396/425 Chevelle 300. Like a lightning bolt coming down from the sky, Bob called Mark and got Mike on the phone to relay the story. Mark's response was, "I need directions to your house."

Mark confirmed that Mike's car was in fact the lone COPO 9719. Jim Mattison, another historian and COPO expert, validated via the Tonawanda production plant that a lone 396/425 was applied to a 1965 Chevelle 300 to further verify the car's authenticity.

In 2019, Mike had the car fully restored by Chevelle restoration professional Doug Garrett. The car will be passed down to Mike's sons.

Legacy

There's an old saying, "It's not *what* you know, it's *who* you know." Was Eddie's career at GM and possible relationship with Bunkie Knudsen the catalyst for the creation of this authentically true 1 of 1 muscle car? With Eddie being gone for more than 30 years, we'll likely never know. But, if he has his old 1965 COPO car in the drag strip in the sky, we'd likely never be able to catch him to ask.

1967 SHELBY GT500 CONVERTIBLE #0139

By Brian Styles

This car was precisely restored to how #0139 was originally made by Shelby American in early December 1966. (Photo Courtesy Al Rogers, Freeze Frame Image LLC)

When it comes to most of the rare ragtops that exist today, each car's rarity is often a direct result of the factory only building the exact quantity that was special-ordered by eager buyers who were visiting dealerships. Convertibles with expensive, powerful engines were not what dealers inventoried with the hope that a local resident would walk in and choose the most expensive and impractical car in the lot. For this one-off ragtop, that is not the case.

Hopes and Dreams

Although Shelby American struggled with the launch of the 1965 GT350, it made up for it in 1966. The company was saved by Ford when it strongly encouraged Hertz Rental Car to purchase 1,000 GT350 units. The resulting profit of 1966 almost exactly made up for the financial loss incurred in 1965. However, because of the illusion of a successful trajectory, Shelby American decided to expand its plans for the 1967 model year. In addition to the high-performance 289-ci 4-barrel GT350, a GT500 with a 428-ci 2x4-barrel Special Interceptor engine was introduced. Next, the Mustang's body was augmented with lightweight fiberglass to give Shelby's GT its own distinct styling to further separate it from the Ford Mustang on which it was based.

The aggressive plan included a convertible bodystyle for the spring of 1967 (1967½), and consideration was being given to offer a hardtop coupe. The future looked so bright that Shelby expanded the 1967 VIN from 11 to 13 digits in anticipation of customer demand being so strong that more than 9,999 total units would be produced.

Shelby American began placing orders on August 8, 1966, which was about 10 days before Mustang production commenced at Ford's San Jose assembly plant.

As part of the preproduction orders, a trio of special Candy Apple Red GT500s (a fastback, coupe, and convertible) were requisitioned for public relations duty. These three GT500s were fully optioned with air conditioning, California emissions, an AM radio, and deluxe Mag Star wheels. There were also 8 fastback units ordered for various engineering and testing roles, and 100 GT350 4-speed units for the showrooms of North American franchise Shelby dealers and to seed initial retail inventory.

As a Shelby American GT	
Shelby GT500 Coupe #0131	**Shelby GT500 Convertible #0139**
The only 1967 GT500 coupe built.	The only 1967 GT convertible built.
The only GT500 coupe built by Shelby American.	The only GT500 convertible built by Shelby American.
The only GT coupe ordered with and factory equipped with dual-quad carburetors.	The only GT convertible ordered with and factory equipped with dual-quad carburetors.
The second GT500 to be serialized and completed by Shelby.	The third GT500 to be serialized and completed by Shelby.

As a Ford Mustang	
Shelby GT500 Coupe #0131	**Shelby GT500 Convertible #0139**
The only multi-carbureted Mustang coupe ever built by Ford.	The only multi-carbureted Mustang convertible ever built by Ford.
The only 1967 Mustang coupe factory equipped with a 428 engine.	The only 1967 Mustang convertible factory equipped with a 428 engine.
The first Mustang coupe to receive a 428 engine.	The first Mustang convertible to receive a 428 engine.
The third Mustang (all bodystyles) with a 428 engine to be serialized by Ford.	The second Mustang (all bodystyles) with a 428 engine to be serialized by Ford.
The second Mustang (all bodystyles) with a 428 engine to be completed by Ford.	The third Mustang (all bodystyles) with a 428 engine to be completed by Ford.

The Best Laid Plans

The first setback to Shelby production came as a result of serious fitment struggles with the improperly formed fiberglass components when attempting to mate them to the knock-down Mustang units that were sent to Shelby's airport facility from the Ford San Jose assembly plant.

Next, Ford was late in building the 428-8V-equipped units. The GT500's new California emissions system hadn't been certified yet. These Ford delays meant that there were no GT500 units at dealerships for the country-wide launch event on November 10, 1966.

Finally Constructed

The GT500 fastback was expedited and built by the San Jose plant on November 7. The GT500 coupe was built the following day on November 8, and the GT500 convertible was built on November 21, 1966. Shelby received serial number 67413C9A00139 (#0139) in the same livery as the other fastbacks completed at that time. Paperwork recorded the car's completion date as December 7, 1966.

As if things couldn't get worse, the trio of air-conditioned GT500s (fastback #0100, coupe #0131, and convertible #0139) were critically overheating.

The overheating issue was eventually solved by changing the location of the grille-mounted high beams, adding ventilation louvers to the hood, adding an oil cooler to the lower grille opening, and converting to an aluminum compressor housing.

Even with its best effort, problems that plagued the 1967 launch ultimately resulted in the midyear convertible being pushed back until the following model year.

Despite thousands of cars being planned, this unfortunate chain of events resulted in Shelby American's first 1967 GT500 convertible being the only 1967 GT convertible ever built. It also meant that Ford's first 428-8V Mustang convertible went down in history as the only multi-carbureted Mustang convertible ever built.

Still Optimistic About the Future

Around the time the plans for a midyear 1967 GT convertible were put out to pasture, Shelby and Ford continued to develop and test their ideas for the 1968-model-year vehicles. It appears that all engineering cars were fitted with louvered hoods, high beams were moved to the outside corners of the grille, and wood grain was applied over the deluxe interior's brushed-aluminum panels. Power-wise for 1968, Shelby considered a GT500 with a 427-4V engine while both companies developed a plan to offer fuel-injected and supercharged models for the upcoming Shelby Cobra GT350 and GT500.

Engineering fastback #0544 received a lightweight 427-ci 4-barrel engine, headers, a chrome grille, and a racing stripe down the center. The only GT500 coupe (#0131) received a formal vinyl roof, brightwork around the grille, and an argent taillight panel, and it was supercharged initially with twin blowers for the dual 4-barrels. Then, it was later reduced to a single 4-barrel with a single blower. The lone 1967 convertible (#0139) received a fiberglass speedster-style landau cap with integral headrests that covered the rear seating compartment.

The End of an Era

Despite its best efforts, the Shelby program continued to struggle financially. Shelby American placed its last fulfilled orders with Ford in March 1967 and continued to develop its 1968 vision into April.

Around the same time, Ford Motor Company decided to call in its note and acquired Shelby American on May 1, 1967. When it did, Ford discarded most of Shelby's incremental vision for the 1968 models and went with its own in-house styling design for the cars. A.O.

This car was updated with Ford's newly designed fiberglass to serve as a "1968 photographic car." The fiberglass components were fabricated by A.O. Smith Plastics in Ionia, Michigan, and were shipped to California circa May 1967. (Photo Courtesy Shelby Research Group Archives)

Because most magazine articles and advertising photos were still published in black and white, the convertible was repainted Wimbledon White. Circa June 1967, #0139 is photographed in front of the exclusive Turf Club at the Hollywood Park horse track. (Photo Courtesy Shelby Research Group Archives)

Smith Plastics was tasked with fabricating two sets of fiberglass front ends, hoods, taillight panels, and center consoles that were shipped to California.

In May and June of 1967, Shelby was tasked with fitting the 1968 fiberglass to a fastback and convertible for photographic purposes. Of course, #0139 was the only convertible on hand, so it was repurposed as a 1968 advertising car. The repurposed fastback was another

With the California operation concluded, engineering vehicles (including #0139) were shipped to Dearborn, Michigan, in August 1967. During the 1968 calendar year, Ford loaned the disguised 1967 convertible to the Alma, Michigan–based Leonard Oil Company for promotional purposes. This photo was taken at the start of the SCCA's Press on Regardless Rally in November 1968.

engineering car (#0463) repainted in Acapulco Blue. Car #0139 was photographed in its original Candy Apple Red paint and then repainted Wimbledon White and photographed at some iconic Southern California locations.

Vehicle production at the Los Angeles airport facility concluded by the end of July. In August, the fixed assets and company vehicles, including this GT500 convertible (#0139), were shipped to Ionia, Michigan, along with a skeleton crew of engineers to start the newly formed Shelby Automotive Company.

Eventually, #0139 (titled as a 1967 model yet still disguised as a 1968) was sold through the Ford dealer network and ended up in the Chicago area. Here is a photo of how #0139 looked when it was owned by Greg Shimkus in the early 1970s. (Photo Courtesy Gregory Shimkus)

During the 1968 calendar year, the 1967 Shelby GT500 convertible (#0139), still disguised as a Wimbledon White 1968, was moved into Ford's marketing department and tagged as oil company promotion with Ray Geddes as the responsible party. It was determined that the oil company was none other than Alma, Michigan's own Leonard Oil Company that used #0139 along with another white 1968 GT500KR convertible in various promotional motorsports activities, such as the SCCA-sanctioned Press on Regardless Rally.

The Present

As the 1969 Shelby program unfolded, the now-outdated 1967 and 1968 cars were sold off.

In the spring of 1969, the first GT500 fastback (#0100) and the only GT500 Coupe (#0131), along with four other engineering units, were sold to Courtesy Motors in Littleton, Colorado, to be unceremoniously sold to the public as used cars.

Although no invoice has been found, it is possible that the lone 1967 GT500 convertible (#0139) was disposed of in the same way. It's also possible it was sold to a Ford employee or to the Leonard Oil Company. All we know is that #0139 remained in the greater Chicago area until it was acquired in 2009 by its present caretakers, Samantha and Brian Styles. The Styles continue to research the company and car's history, although the ownership trail has stalled at identifying the owner from 1969 to 1971, who is reported to have resided in the town of Addison, Illinois.

The present caretakers are still researching the early private ownership of #0139 from 1969 to 1971, which was presumably in the Chicago suburbs. If you can help or you just want to read more about this car, visit 1967shelbyconvertible.com. (Photo Courtesy Al Rogers, Freeze Frame Image LLC)

1967 PLYMOUTH BELVEDERE II HEMI FOUR-DOOR

By Matti Färm

This staged barn-find display of the lone 1967 Belvedere II four-door Hemi car is perfectly fitting. The fact the car is in Finland is even better. (Photo Courtesy Jan Richardsson)

As of the late 1960s, Finland was a notoriously poor country with not much American iron being imported. Most of the cars funneled into the country were smaller vehicles, such as VWs, Fiats, Minis, and other European cars.

However, by a magical stroke of luck, the land of a thousand lakes was able to haul in one of the rarest Mopars ever to grace Europe: a 1967 Plymouth Belvedere II four-door with a Hemi.

Checking the Right Boxes

Arne Berner had the upper hand in ordering cars, as he was the Finnish importer for Plymouths and Chryslers. He was a family friend of Ottar Bingen, the manager of Scandinavian Chrysler. Bingen had a 1966 Satellite with a 383, which was the largest official engine available in the Belvedere models for Finnish buyers. Berner test-drove

Bingen's Satellite and liked it a lot. Bingen knew that Berner liked fast cars and told him that there were even more powerful engines than the 383.

With Berner being a modest family man, he wanted to order a humble-looking four-door car. He didn't know that something like this wasn't the norm in the States, so Berner ordered a 426 Hemi into an otherwise basic four-door Belvedere II—and with that order, a legend was born.

Hemi Four Doors

Back in the United States, Chrysler opened the can of worms for four-door 426 Hemis in 1966. Across the street at Dodge, it is estimated that five 426 mills were dropped into Coronet Deluxe sedans during the calendar year. Allegedly, one car went to Canada, one went outside of North America, and three stayed in the country. All five of the cars received Chrysler's TorqueFlite automatic transmission and had Sure-Grip 8¾ rear ends with the base 3.23 gears.

The Finnish Hemi Plymouth was ordered in AA1 Silver Poly paint and featured a blue bench seat interior with a column-shift Torque-Flite, 8¾ rear end, and a 3.23 Sure-Grip. The only other options on the II were the passenger-side mirror, clock, power steering, and power disc brakes. Remember, Berner was modest! The Hemi badges on the

Arne Berner is the person responsible for the creation and importing of the 1967 Hemi Belvedere II. Arne used the car in an advertising video for the new cars in Finland for 1967. (Photo Courtesy Arne Berner)

fenders were the only thing out of the ordinary on the Belvedere II. Now, if you popped the hood, that's a different story.

Delivery Day

Berner's Hemi arrived in Finland in January 1967 and was his daily driver in Helsinki. He had a heavy foot, and there were no speed limits in Finland at that time. It's been reported that the 200-kph speedometer (125 mph) was buried many times. With 3.23 gears and an underrated 425 hp, the only thing that kept Berner from reaching stock car speeds were the winding roads.

One time, Berner was driving home with his friend and had the speedometer buried at 200 kph. His friend was a little scared and nervously said to Berner, "Yeah, this is really fast car."

Berner looked over, said, "Wait, there is more," and pushed the pedal to the metal.

Berner had a summer cottage in eastern Finland, and many times the clock was started at home and stopped at the cottage. It was a constant challenge to improve his time each trip. Berner's son remembered that the trips to the cottage took so much longer with his mother's Simca 1000 compared to his father's Plymouth. There was one close call on the way home. Someone coming from the opposite direction turned left in front of Berner, and he had to hit the ditch to dodge the potential crash. The car survived with minor damage. The near-collision may have been the catalyst for Berner to finally sell the big-block brute. In May 1968, the Belvedere was sold to a new owner.

Hemi Hoarder: Second Owner

There were only two Hemi cars that were ordered new in Finland. Amazingly, the new owner of the Belvedere had previously ordered a 1967 Plymouth GTX and now possessed both Hemis. What good is one if it can't have a friend, right?

Before his Hemis, this owner had a Plymouth with a slant six that didn't have enough power when it came time to make a timely pass on the Finnish roads. One close call with an oncoming truck was enough for him and was the primary reason he wanted a Hemi in the first place. He had a heavy foot just like Berner. The 60-mile trip from Helsinki to Hämeenlinna took only 35 minutes!

For the new owner, the Belvedere was an all-season driver. He had the old-fashioned habit of using water for coolant and drained it when temperatures dropped below freezing. Unfortunately, one night, he forgot to drain the water, and the original block cracked beyond repair. A new short-block was installed, and the Belvedere changed hands again in July 1969.

The Third Owner

In 1973, the Belvedere wound up on a used car lot after it was traded for a new Dodge Monaco. Apparently, the new owner needed a fast car to run from the cops. If that doesn't sound American enough for the Belvedere, I don't know what does!

There were several times when the extra speed was needed. One time, the owner was coming from eastern Finland with a trunk full of illegal booze. Someone had warned the police, and they were waiting for him with a Porsche and souped-up Volvo. The Hemi Belvedere ran through a roadblock, and the chase was on! Allegedly, the Hemi Belvedere driver slowed down so that the police could catch up, waved from his window, floored it, and got away. The mischievous owner was alleged to have boxes of ceiling nails in the back seat and would throw a box out of the window to bring the law to a grinding halt. There are rumors that the car was used in bank robberies too.

The third owner never was caught, but he crashed the car in early 1974. He had gone off the road, hit a big rock, and mangled the front bumper, fender, and radiator. The passenger-side quarter panel was damaged as well. Thankfully, this ended the Bonnie-and-Clyde era for the Hemi Plymouth.

Fourth Owner

In March 1974, Kaj Svensson bought the car. His father worked at a Finnish Dodge importer and had ordered a 1970 Challenger with a Six Pack, so they were familiar with the big engines from Mopar. Svensson repaired the front-end and quarter-panel damage. He pulled the Hemi and got new bearings and piston rings.

Unfortunately, the aesthetics of a four-door sedan wasn't a cool bodystyle for Svensson, who noted that it resembled a boxy taxicab. Back then, it was a base Belvedere with a big engine. No one knew how rare it was. Svensson had also bought a 1967 Charger, and one day after work, he drove both cars to a do-it-yourself garage. The next morning, the powertrains were swapped, and the Belvedere received a 318 engine with a 904 TorqueFlite transmission. Svensson sold both cars before he joined the army.

Hiding in Plain Sight

After that, the Belvedere was passed around, and no one understood how special it was. In September 1976, the Belvedere moved to central Finland, where two brothers owned it. In the late 1970s, the 318 was pulled and painted bright red along with the rear end. New brake lines, which were also painted red, were added along with a set of Cragars. The rear end was raised, and leopard-pattern seat covers were installed.

In September 1984, the Plymouth was sold and moved to Southern Lapland, where it went through a few more owners and had a quiet life.

The Hunt Is On

Jan Richardsson learned of Max Wedge and Hemi engines from Swedish magazines as a teenager in the late 1970s. When he learned of this car in the early 1980s, he was determined to find it. Back then, it was not easy to search for cars, and Richardsson didn't even know its license-plate number. But after several years of searching, he found it in Southern Lapland in April 1986.

Richardsson owned a nice 1965 Coronet with a big-block at that time. He took the Coronet, some cash, and made an offer on the Belvedere. The car was in need of a brake job, so Richardsson got the parts and completed the project in the soon-to-be former owner's driveway. About 300 miles later, Richardsson pulled the Belvedere into his driveway and his long search was over.

Richardsson enjoyed the Belvedere and racked up tens of thousands of miles over the decade that he owned the car. In 1994, he took the Belvedere to the Vantaa Happy Days Car Show and displayed it as a barn find. This is where Seppo Piki saw the Belvedere for the first time. He got to know Richardsson and inquired about purchasing the Belvedere, but it was not for sale.

In May 1998, Richardsson and Piki were at the same car show again. Piki found Richardsson and asked what his plans were for the Belvedere and if it was for sale. Surprisingly, Richardsson said that it

Without its Hemi emblems, the Belvedere II is an unassuming daily driver that can trounce nearly anything. (Photo Courtesy Jan Richardsson)

could be sold. Piki replied, "I'll take it!"

A deal was made, and a few weeks later, Piki got the car home. The car was more run down since the 1994 show, as neighbor kids had smashed all of the headlights and taillights, but, luckily, nothing else was broken.

Over the years, Piki has found many NOS parts, taillights, the trunk panel, headlight bezels, side moldings, the radiator, and other parts. Another Hemi has been built for the Belvedere too.

Piki managed to find the original transmission, which had found its way into a 1970 Hemi 'Cuda. To get the numbers-matching transmission from out of the 'Cuda, he had to find that car's original transmission, and wouldn't you know, he did!

Lasting Legacy

From its modest beginnings with Bingen, through its current caretaker Piki, it's fair to say this Plymouth has a story like no other. Piki plans to conduct a full concours restoration on the Belvedere. With only one 1967 Plymouth Belvedere II four-door with a Hemi accounted for, there's no question that this machine should be considered one of Finland's greatest landmarks. Northern lights be damned!

1968 Z/28 PETE ESTES CONVERTIBLE

by BK Nakadashi

Chevrolet President Pete Estes was believed to have liked convertibles. Designer life becomes much easier when you can homologate parts and create something nice for the boss. (Photo Courtesy David Newhardt/Mecum Auctions)

When you run the largest division of the largest car company on earth, a division that was once so big that the federal government investigated whether it should be broken away from its parent company in presumed violation of anti-trust laws, you can pretty much get what you want. You can get things that aren't supposed to exist.

In the days before big-block COPOs, a Z/28 was as hardcore of a Camaro that you could get at the local dealership. Its shivery idle and downright nasty demeanor was something tolerated only by a limited number of people. It was an image car and was something designed to bolster every other Camaro that rolled out of the showroom. At the time that this was written, the Corvette was scheduled to receive a sedan and an SUV as part of its lineup by 2025.

Trans-Am Racing

As the SCCA Trans-Am wars heated up, Chevy became serious about making a homologation package to run in the series.

The cross-ram intake manifold with a pair of 585-cfm carburetors was on the agenda for homologation purposes. (Photo Courtesy David Newhardt/Mecum Auctions)

Legendarily, Chevy's package was called the Z/28. It was a Camaro so serious that Chevy's marketing department couldn't think of a proper name for it and left the alphanumeric RPO code as its nomenclature.

For $358, Chevy loaded its new-for-1967 Camaro with F41 heavy-duty suspension, quicker steering, 15-inch Rally wheels on 7.35-15 tires, snazzy stripes on the hood and trunk, and a special engine that combined the 283 small-block's shorter-stroke crank with the 327's bigger-bore block. This combination came out to 302 ci, a magic number that fell just under the SCCA's 5-liter displacement limit. Mandatory Z/28 options included the close-ratio 4-speed transmission and power-assisted front disc brakes.

Other than an automatic transmission, air conditioning, and convertible roofline, America at large could get anything it wanted on a Z/28. As a unibody car that was designed for the nation's winding road courses, such as Road America and Watkins Glen, it needed its roof for structural rigidity. A convertible may have been marginally lighter, but even with a roll bar, chassis flex would be unmanageable (and slow) under the stresses of a race. Ragtops were in opposition to the purpose of the Z/28.

One for Pete

Pete Estes liked convertibles. He ran Chevy from 1965 to 1972, during the height of the muscle-car era. If two million units are shipped a year, is it too much for someone in engineering to approve a convertible version of a car that doesn't have a convertible version on the order form? It is not.

Vince Piggins ran Chevy's racing activities at the time and coordinated the Z/28 program for the SCCA. He had some parts that he wanted to get homologated and needed the boss's okay. There's a difference between seeing numbers on a spreadsheet and feeling what those components can do in a car. Piggins inquired as to whether a Z/28 convertible was possible.

After Piggins was given the go-ahead, in July 1968, he ordered a single Fathom Green ragtop through Chevy's fleet special order department, which is also where the legendary COPO cars came from. The resulting ride, as you might expect of an executive-level car, was no street rat. Positraction, an AM/FM stereo, auxiliary gauges in the console, power windows, a tilt wheel, folding rear seat, rear-window defroster, and more were all on board.

Styling Exercise

Once it was built, the only first-generation Z/28 convertible was quietly redirected to the GM tech center in Warren, Michigan, for the installation of a handful of parts that Piggins was keen to get approval for. This included a cross-ram intake manifold with twin 585-cfm carburetors, a fiberglass cowl plenum (essentially a prototype of the piece that appears on 1969 models) to help force-feed those two carburetors, four-wheel disc brakes (a mid-1969 RPO that became known as JL8 among Camaro cognoscenti), performance suspension beyond GM's highly-regarded F41, Koni shocks, and headers.

Then, just as quietly, the Camaro was delivered to the executive garage for Estes's use. What better way to win approval for homologating parts than to install them on the boss's car to see how he liked them?

While the Camaro was one car of many in his rotation, period reports have Estes driving it more often than just about anything else that was offered to him in the six months that it was available. Piggins received the approval that he sought. With costs sorted out and

The cowl-induction hood had to wait another year before it found a home on the Camaro. However, those thirsty cross-ram carburetors were happy that this hood could feed them. (Photo Courtesy David Newhardt/Mecum Auctions)

the parts approved for the production of the 1969 Camaro Z/28, and actual 1969 model cars available for Estes to drive, this 1 of 1 Z/28 convertible was quietly divested of its special components.

Once the car was brought back to as stock as a first-generation Z/28 convertible can be, it was sold through Bill Markley Chevrolet, the division's preferred dealer for selling off cars that came out of the executive fleet. It was conveniently located within sight of the GM building's front door.

Ownership History

The ownership chain of this 1 of 1 is known from new. GM employee T.H. Standen bought it from the dealership and was technically its first owner.

Two years later, he sold it to a coworker, Vern Nye, who held onto it for almost two decades. Car auctioneer Dana Mecum found it in the late 1980s, had it restored, and sold it for what was then a record of $172,000 in 1991. It was purchased by Milt Robson, whose name is well-known in muscle-car collector circles.

After a short stint under the ownership of the Rock 'n Roll Toy Store in Highland Park, Illinois, it was purchased by Al Maynard. His ownership was important for a few reasons. He had sourced all of the correct racing components that were part and parcel of what Estes experienced, and he commissioned Supercar Specialties' Scott Tiemann to do some additional restoration work.

In 2004, the car was due to be sold at auction but failed to meet its $1 million reserve. Instead, Dana Mecum overcame his seller's regret and purchased it back. It remains in his collection today.

This car's significance is twofold. First, it was the only one built, and its history and legend make it a remarkable bit of business in its own right. But also consider that it was a test mule for the 1969 Camaro Z/28 and Chevy's SCCA exploits for the 1969 season.

It's fair to say that for Chevrolet, and particularly Roger Penske's team running Camaros, it was a fantastic year for the bowtie brand on America's road courses. It took home 8 wins out of 12 races, although only the best 9 races counted. The Camaro never finished off the podium for the year. Penske pilot Mark Donohue took the bulk of the victories, although Ron Bucknum won Mid-Ohio and Seattle. The Z/28 was so successful on that track that Chevrolet could have sat out its last race at Riverside and still clinched the over-2-liter championship in the SCCA Trans-Am series.

A first-generation Z/28 convertible was not supposed to exist, but at the tail end of the 1960s, the car that wasn't supposed to exist made Chevrolet and Z/28 Camaros better.

The Pete Estes Z/28 convertible checks a lot of boxes. With its rear spoiler, bumper guards, and wheel lip molding, there's plenty of sizzle with the steak. (Photo Courtesy David Newhardt/Mecum Auctions)

1968 FORD SHELBY COBRA GT500KR

By Ed Dedick

Royal Maroon wasn't a paint option on a 1968 Shelby GT500 KR. However, it is if you are Carroll Shelby's special lady. (Photo Courtesy the American Muscle Car Museum)

The initials "KR" that were added to Shelby Mustang GT500s were more than just letters. As legend has it, the King of the Road name was swiped from a General Motors project, and Carroll Shelby quickly capitalized on it with the new GT500KR. You snooze, you lose, right?

The 1968 Shelby Cobra GT500KR became a midyear introduction for Shelby and was based on the 1968 GT500. With the slogan, "Buy it or watch it go by," Ford added "Cobra" to the Shelby's nameplate to help introduce the beginning of a new performance era at the company and borrowed the moniker from its ever popular and successful British race cars.

For 1968, Shelby production relocated to the Ford plant in Ionia, Michigan, under direct supervision from George Merwin of Ford Motor Company. Ford's intention was to increase production of the Shelby cars for 1968.

Unfortunately, with the move and a production strike by the United Auto Workers at the plant during the model year, only a total of 1,571 1968 Shelby Cobra GT500KRs were constructed, with 518 being convertibles. The first year for Shelby convertibles was 1968, sans the lone 1967 car that is featured in this book. The Ford 427 Cobra Roadster was gone from production this year.

Cobra Jet

The Cobra nameplate referred to Ford's R-code 428 Cobra Jet V-8, which was underrated at 335 hp. It was the Cobra Jet's first appearance in a Shelby, which created the catalyst for the new King of the Road moniker. The 428 Cobra Jet replaced the 428 Police Interceptor engine that was previously outfitted. The Cobra Jet motor included revised 427 low-rise heads, stronger internals, Cobra Le Mans finned valve covers, and a dual-plane intake manifold with a 735-cfm Holley 4-barrel carburetor to feed this Shelby powerplant. All of this resided under the custom fiberglass hood that featured a fiberglass-chambered fitting that sent outside air directly to the air cleaner. These hoods had custom self-retained push-and-turn hood locks. Additionally, the Cobra Jet cars received heavy front and rear shocks. The 4-speed cars had staggered rear shocks. A new "428 COBRA JET" logo adorned the front fenders as well.

Royal Maroon

Production colors for 1968 Shelby GT500KRs were Raven Black, Acapulco Blue, Lime Gold, Wimbledon White, Highland Green, Candy Apple Red, Fleet Yellow, Dark Blue Metallic, and Gold Metallic. Interior choices were limited to either Black or Saddle. This Shelby is the only ragtop painted in Royal Maroon (Ford paint code 3059A).

Ford applied buck tags on the driver-side inner fender of production models. These tags listed options, and in this case, denoted "MAROON" as the color. (Photo Courtesy the American Muscle Car Museum)

The interior for this car is the Saddle décor interior with bucket seats to create a unique and striking color combination for this 1 of 1.

While Royal Maroon was a new standard color for a 1968 production Mustang, it was not for the Shelby cars. Carroll Shelby had to use his charm and relationship with Henry Ford II to work his magic. The story goes that Henry told Shelby, "Do you know how much it will cost me to stop production to paint this car this color?"

Shelby replied, "Do you know how much it will cost me to get divorced?"

Thus, three of these Shelby GT500KR cars were painted Royal Maroon: two coupes and this convertible.

Happy Wife, Happy Life

The unique aspect of the convertible is that it was Shelby's wife's personal car, and the color was her favorite nail-polish color. From our research, this woman was believed to be Joan Sherman, who was the model in the early Shelby sales and marketing brochures, as well as Shelby's business manager.

It's believed that Carroll Shelby created the 1968 Shelby GT500 KR for his special lady, Joan Sherman. (Photo Courtesy the American Muscle Car Museum)

The 1968 Shelby GT500 KR was the debut of the 428 Cobra Jet engine in the lineup. No expense was spared on this 1 of 1 Mustang. (Photo Courtesy the American Muscle Car Museum)

After this car was first produced with a release date of June 5, 1968, it was listed as being owned by Shelby America for a period of time, which was typical of cars used by Carroll Shelby, his family, and staff members—or for development and testing.

By 1968, Shelby had 111 Ford dealers onboard as Shelby franchises, and 9 of these franchises were located in Canada. In August 1970, this car was sold new through Shelby dealer Frank Cate Ford, which was in Elk Grove, California.

The base price was $4,594.09 for this GT500KR. It was well optioned with power front disc brakes, power steering, a shoulder harness, AM/FM Multiplex radio, Select-O-Matic transmission, SelectAire air conditioning, tinted glass, a Tilt-Pop steering wheel, tachometer, trip odometer, and white power convertible top with glass back light. With the options and shipping included, the final price was $5,648.72.

With the original build sheet and research courtesy of Kevin Marti and Marti Auto Works, along with SAAC documentation, this Shelby is confirmed to be a 1 of 1. It has also undergone a full professional rotisserie restoration and retains its original, numbers-matching drivetrain, and receives continuous maintenance by the experienced staff at the American Muscle Car Museum.

This special Shelby is currently owned by Mark Pieloch. Pieloch is the owner and founder of the American Muscle Car Museum, which is in Melbourne, Florida, where the car is on display for thousands to enjoy every year.

1969 DODGE CHARGER DAYTONA
By Billy and Jennifer Pope

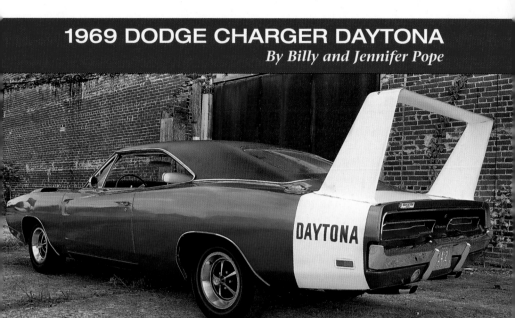

The aero wars of the 1960s are a high point in NASCAR racing. The 1969 Daytona was Dodge's response to the Ford Torinos getting more slippery with their Torino Talladegas and Cyclone Spoiler IIs. (Photo Courtesy Billy Pike)

It began when I was a kid. I always liked the 1960s and 1970s muscle cars. When I was about to turn 16, my parents asked me what kind of car I wanted. I told them, "I want a 1970 Chevelle."

They searched high and low for this car, and they finally found me a 1970 Chevelle SS 396, 4-speed, bench-seat car that was cranberry red with black stripes and black interior. What a great way to begin my muscle-car life. They purchased it on July 4, 1985, and I still have the car to this day.

Car Collecting

This began my love of collecting cars. After many years, I got married, and we started getting serious about car collecting. We bought Chevelles, Camaros, Buicks, Oldsmobiles, and Pontiacs. After I got exactly what I wanted in the General Motors world, I decided to start looking at Mopars.

We were automatically drawn to the wing cars as our favorites. We loved them, but after we began pricing them, we realized that they were out of our reach at that time. We knew we had to climb the financial ladder to get there.

We bought a 1970 Dodge Challenger T/A, and a year later, we got a 1970 Plymouth 'Cuda AAR. These were great cars, and we met a lot of great people while we owned them, but my dream of purchasing a wing car still hadn't been fulfilled.

Wing Car, Where Are You?

We had to come up with a plan to be able to afford a wing car. The only thing we could think of was that we had to sell a few cars to downsize. That was a very hard decision because some of these cars had been in our collection for more than 20 years. It was very bittersweet to see some of these cars leave. With a little cash in our pocket, we started the hunt to find the perfect wing car.

I looked every day on the internet for leads. I messaged, emailed, called, texted, sent Facebook messages, and started going to Mopar shows to find some contacts. After six months of doing this, I finally started to get some positive leads.

We loaded up and headed out on several road trips to look at these cars. We did this for about two years, and each car we looked at wasn't the one for us. We started to get very discouraged that we were never going to find the right one. In September 2020, we found a 1970 Plymouth Superbird that was a Lemon Twist survivor car, so I loaded up the trailer and went to pick it up.

We loved this car and enjoyed it so much, although my aspirations turned to owning a Dodge Daytona, but we couldn't afford to have both wing cars. We had to make a very difficult decision to sell the Superbird to help fund the Daytona.

We had many sleepless nights because we were worried about selling the car and never finding another one. I started the hunt again but looked for a Dodge Daytona this time. We received several leads on Daytonas, but the ones we looked at were still not the one for us. Finally, we got a lead on a 1969 Dodge Daytona that had never been sold, registered, or titled.

An Unregistered Daytona

We couldn't believe it and thought that it was too good to be true. The next task was finding the owner's contact information. After a few weeks, I finally found someone who knew about the car and acquired the owner's phone number. I called the owner, talked with them about the car, and verified this was the Dodge Daytona from Brockton Dodge that had never been sold, registered, or titled.

They confirmed that it was the Daytona from Brockton Dodge, and I told my wife, "I think this is the car we've been dreaming of."

The owner and I talked several times on the phone about the car, and he emailed me all the paperwork so that I could research the car. We decided to plan a trip to go see it in person. We had conflicting schedules. They were going to be on vacation for a month, and when they came back, we were going to be on vacation for two weeks. I was a nervous wreck this whole time and worried that someone else would buy it or the owner would back out of selling the car because he had owned the car for more than 52 years.

During this time, I called and texted the owner several times about the car, so he knew that I was the right buyer for his Daytona and not a tire kicker. I had to hurry up and leave to make this deal happen.

Seeing is Believing

In October 2021, we scheduled a trip to buy the car. I set out on the 16-hour drive (one way) by myself since my wife couldn't go because of work. On the drive down there, all I could think about was that he was going to change his mind and not sell me the car after I showed up.

When I finally got to his house, there it was, sitting in his garage. I was so excited to finally lay my eyes on this 1969 Dodge Daytona. When I got out of the truck, I walked around the car for about 5 minutes. Then, I asked him if he had all the paperwork on the Daytona and he said that he did. We went inside, and he and his wife had it all laying out on the kitchen table for me to view. I looked over all of the paperwork and told him that I would take the car. I had never even driven the car or heard it start.

After the deal was done, I asked him if the car would start so that it could be driven onto the trailer and he said, "No problem." I let him drive it one last time onto the trailer.

After the car was loaded, I called my wife and told her that the car was on the trailer, the deal was done, and I was on my way home. I think she was more excited than I was.

Staying Unregistered

When we got the car home, we were going to get it registered. I talked with several of my car friends and they said not to do it because it would kill the value and history of the car. After all, one of the reasons we wanted this car was because of its history.

We decided not to register it, but then came the next challenge. We had to find an insurance company that would insure it without being registered.

That was a task in itself. We called many insurance companies, and they all said they would not insure the car without it being registered. We didn't know what to do, but we finally found an insurance company that would insure it for us.

Here's a little history on the car.

The manufacturer's statement of origin was March 22, 1969. It was originally shipped from Elm Wood Dodge in Providence, Rhode Island, and was dealer swapped on September 26, 1969, to Brockton Dodge in Massachusetts for the sum of $3,557.32. This car was used at

This 1969 Dodge Daytona still retains its original dealer plate. Why? Because it's never been registered! (Photo Courtesy Billy Pike)

Brockton Dodge as a promotional car to advertise the dealership. The dealership owner loved wing cars and the vinyl tops on the Superbirds, so he had a vinyl top installed on this Daytona, along with the lettering of Brockton Dodge added to the car.

This is 1 of 3 Daytonas that had a dealer-installed vinyl top. The Brockton Dodge dealership installed the vinyl roof on November 21, 1969. More details are below:

- This is a numbers-matching car
- 440 engine, 375 hp
- 727 automatic transmission
- Bucket-seat console car
- Original trim tag
- Factory B5 Blue with white interior
- It has a broadcast sheet and original IBM (production) card from Chrysler
- This car has around 11,000 miles on it
- 1 of 503 Daytonas made
- 1 of 23 B5 Blue cars
- #228 in the Daytona Registry
- The only unregistered Daytona

This car has had one repaint back to its factory color on June 27, 1972, to cover up the billboard lettering of the dealership. It has

Brockton Dodge in Massachusetts used the Daytona for promotional purposes. Here, it sits outside with another winged car: a 1970 Plymouth Superbird. (Photo Courtesy Billy Pike)

never been wrecked and has all original sheet metal. It came with the following options:

- B5 Blue
- A01 Light Group
- D56-3:55 axle package
- B41 front disk brakes
- G16 console
- E86 440 4-barrel carburetor
- G33 left remote-control mirror
- J25 3-speed wipers
- J55 undercoat with hood insulator pad
- R11 Music Master AM radio
- R31 rear seat speaker
- S77 power steering
- S81 Sport Type wood steering wheel
- W21 chrome stamp road wheels with trim rings

We have no intention of ever titling this car, so it will always remain a brand-new 1969 Dodge Daytona. We plan on traveling to several events to display this car because many people have never seen or heard about it.

When we set out to own a winged car, we had no idea that we'd end up with such a unique car. It's an honor for us to be the caretakers, and we hope to share this car with many of you in the future.

1969 PETTY BLUE PLYMOUTH ROAD RUNNER CONVERTIBLE

By Bill Adams Jr.

Petty Blue has been around since the 1950s. In 2019, Richard Petty told Dale Earnhardt Jr., "We didn't have enough paint to paint the car. So, we grabbed some white paint, and we had some blue paint, and we just poured it all together." (Photo Courtesy Bill Adams)

We all have stories of the cars that got away: those rare barn/garage/field finds that we passed up, watched someone else buy, or picked up and sold off quickly to make ends meet.

This is the one Road Runner that couldn't escape Wile E. Coyote or Bill Adams Jr. This is the story of my 1969 Plymouth Road Runner convertible. It's a factory 99 paint code Petty Blue car with a white deluxe interior, a console 4-speed, and a 383 engine. This is the only convertible known to exist that was ever painted Petty Blue from the factory.

Bill Adams Sr.

First, some background. My father, Bill Adams Sr., was an icon in the hobby. He was on the founding board of directors of the Walter P.

Chrysler (WPC) Club for Chryslers in 1968. In 1974, he became the second president of the club, and I am now the current president.

I had the good fortune to grow up in the Bay Area in central California when it was easy to get around and there were wonderful places to go touring with your car. Every weekend was some sort of car or club activity. My ride home, fresh off the assembly line in 1970, was a 1939 Chrysler Royal Windsor Hayes coupe that I still own. Unfortunately, my father is now roaming the rows of cars in his favorite wrecking yards in heaven. I will miss him forever and see him again.

Road Runners for Sale

In 1998, I was living in Troutdale, Oregon. I had been living in Rhode Island for a few years to go to college and work after I got out of the U.S. Navy. The internet was quickly becoming a great way to score some deals on cars and parts. One day, I came across an ad for two Road Runners that were in a ditch in central California, smack in the middle of gold-rush country. They were reasonably priced, but details were minimal. One was a convertible 1969 Road Runner, and the other was a coupe. Since I knew people in the area, I asked a friend to go look at them for me. His response to me after he checked them out was, "Well, if you don't buy them, I'm going to." That was enough for me.

I recruited my friend Jeff Wiford to take his truck and trailer to California and buy the cars. When we finally got to the site, the cars were down in a ditch off a private driveway. The property owner was frustrated that his friend left these cars on his property years before and had pushed them into a drainage ditch off his driveway. Fortunately, the convertible hit a small tree a few feet from the bottom of the ditch and rested on an incline.

Over the years, the water in the ditch dried out and left the floors, trunk floor, and quarters in perfect condition. Other than typical surface rust, the car had no weak spots. Plus, all of the convertible-only stuff was still there. The white top had been left halfway up, and leaves filled the car. Once they were cleaned out, they surprisingly hadn't created any rust.

I didn't really think of the color at the time; only that it was odd.

As everybody knows, where there is a will, there is a way, and we finally got both Road Runners out of the ditch with a lot of

It's hard to understand why a person would push a car into a ravine. It's very fortunate for this 1969 Road Runner convertible that it wasn't exposed to salted roads prior to finding itself near water. (Photo Courtesy Bill Adams)

MacGyvering and hair-brained ideas that actually worked. We made arrangements to store the coupe at my friend's property nearby, and I took the convertible home. Once I got home, I began, for the first time, to try and figure out what exactly I had.

What Did I Buy?

Once I decoded the fender tag, it didn't take long to determine that the 99 paint code was very unique. I began to look around and compare the color to available special-order colors. At that time, Petty Blue was regarded as a very rare color. There were only whispers of Petty Blue Road Runners prior to 1971.

There were a few pictures of 1971 Road Runners and other Chrysler products with paint code TB3, Basin Street Blue/Corporate Blue, that was used in 1971 and later. However, the more I dug, the more I suspected it was a factory Petty Blue car.

I crawled all over the trunk area and into the rear, undercarriage, floors, and even under the dash. I could find no evidence of a repaint or any other color. I did as much research as possible, only to come back to my original hypothesis that this was indeed an original Petty

Blue car. I decided to keep the original decklid for color matching and to authenticate its originality. It is hanging on the wall in my shop.

I became infatuated with the car and all things Petty Blue and vowed to never part with it, no matter the cost. I slowly began to amass the parts to put it back together. Life also happened.

Waiting is the Hardest Part

It sat in my garage in my first house in Oregon for a few years. I cleaned it up and collected parts. Then came a job change and a move to Carson City, Nevada. I took the car with me and didn't have storage for it, so it sat outside, and I covered it the best that I could. The job opportunity wasn't what it was supposed to be, so times got a bit rough.

I was offered $15,000 for the car as it sat in early 2001. Times were tough, and it would have solved a lot of problems, but thankfully I was still single and only had myself to worry about. I again resolved that even if I had to live in the darned thing, I would not sell it, and I damn near had to.

Things got better and my career began to flourish again. My father and I bought some property in Dayton, Nevada, and moved the car out there. I finally began to put the car together. However, as things heated up in the world, I was called back to military service and had to leave for a while.

Upon my return, I again needed some help, and an easy option was to sell the car. By now, the offers were higher than $15,000. My earlier resolve stayed firm, and I dug in my heels to find other alternatives.

Another military branch actively recruited me and promised a bonus upon entering the program. Just as I was about to sign up, I met the woman who is now my wife in the chow hall on a base—of all places. We were both in the reserves, and I re-evaluated my options. I ended up in California with a better job opportunity that was near to her. The Road Runner followed me back to California. It was fairly close to where I had originally pulled it out of a ditch.

I took the fender tag to Chrysler Performance West's Spring Fling show in 2004, where I presented it to Mopar historian Galen Govier. He took a picture of the tag, and I ordered his research service on the car. Later, I got a letter back from him that confirmed my suspicions. He found no record of any other Petty Blue convertible Road Runner, and for that matter, no record of any other convertible ever painted Petty Blue.

Time to Restore

As time wore on, my job flourished, as did my family. I finally had the means to start work on the Road Runner. I generally do most of my own mechanical work, but bodywork is another story. After investigating a few places, I opted for one that specialized in classics. This was around 2007, which was roughly 10 years after I acquired the car.

The business of classic car restoration and bodywork is unfortunately riddled with issues. As such, the Road Runner ended up in three different shops before any progress was made. We have all heard the horror stories of cars disappearing from the restoration shop, so I was determined that would not happen to my car. I visited the shop and car every few weeks to ensure that it went nowhere. There was some progress each month, but it was minimal.

The years ticked by, and the progress was grindingly slow on the Road Runner. The bodywork was partially done, and the front panels were ready for paint. The silver lining of the slow process was being able to see the condition of the original body panels. No rust beyond the surface ever materialized.

Interesting History

In about 2016, I found out Wes Eisenschenk was writing a book on 1969 Road Runners. I sent him a copy of my fender tag, and he contacted me right away. Eisenschenk was able to confirm a few other interesting facts. It was built mere days before Richard Petty's defection to Ford for most of the 1969 year. Supposedly, Petty didn't like the non-aero 1968 and 1969 Road Runners and wanted a Daytona. Allegedly, Plymouth said, "No. You drive for Plymouth, not Dodge."

Bad move, Mopar. He came right back with the Superbird.

Eisenschenk also verified that the inspection stamps and options were correct for the car. Amazingly, he found a classified ad in the *Sacramento Bee* on April 17, 1969, that showed the Road Runner sold when it was new at Vanderberg Chrysler Plymouth Imperial. About that same time, I received a call from Galen Govier with an offer from a buyer in Florida who wanted factory Petty Blue cars. Sorry, not for sale.

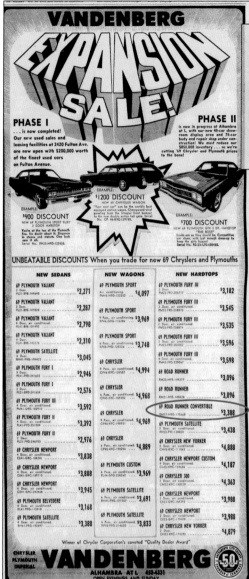

A VIN search on newspapers.com yielded an incredible find: a selling dealership! The Petty Blue convertible was listed in the Sacramento Bee *on April 17, 1969. (Images Courtesy* Sacramento Bee)

Family First

In 2019, life threw us a serious curveball. Since its inception in 2002, my family has helped with a car show in Las Vegas. Originally known as Mopars at the Strip, it is now called Muscle Cars at the Strip. We have been regular attendees, and we help with judging, parking, coordination, and whatever is needed.

My son Luke began regularly accompanying me to the show when he was 9 years old. Luke was diagnosed with high-functioning autism at age 3 and was a fairly normal kid who loved cars, especially Road Runners.

At the event in April 2019, Luke was very lethargic and didn't want to get out of the 1966 Chrysler 300 convertible that we had driven to the meet. I knew something was wrong. I immediately took him home and to the doctor, whose response based on Luke's blood results was, "I don't know how he is even upright. You're going to the emergency room immediately."

Bill Adams's children enjoy some fun out of the sun in the drop-top bird. It was Luke who inspired the show The Ride That Got Away *to feature the Road Runner. (Photo Courtesy Bill Adams)*

Within a few hours, Luke was airlifted to Valley Children's Hospital in Madera, California. His diagnosis was leukemia. It's every parent's worst nightmare. We nearly lost him three times, but he did what I asked of him and fought valiantly each time. As a parent who can do nothing but watch, pray, and hope, it means more than people know when friends, family, and even strangers offer their sincere thoughts and prayers.

For one year we were in and out of the hospital for treatment and recurring illnesses while Luke underwent chemotherapy. We were physically in the hospital for almost five months of the year. Luke has made a complete recovery and is trying to catch up with a few lost years of his life and development.

During all of this time, the Road Runner was still in the back of my mind. It was also the first time I acknowledged that if I had to sell the car to take care of my son, I would.

A few friends and some strangers rallied to Luke's cause unbeknownst to me. Many of my friends knew about my Road Runner. For reasons I still can't fully comprehend, they decided they were going to help finish the Road Runner as an aid to Luke's recovery.

The Ride That Got Away . . . Kind of

Most of us in the car world know who Courtney Hansen is. She has hosted many car shows on different networks. She was the celebrity at the Mopars at the Strip show in 2014 and 2015. Luke hung out with her every chance he got, and I can't say that I blame him.

Hansen was very gracious and understanding with him. She signed a hat for Luke that he wore until his mother made it disappear because it was falling apart.

Hansen's new show was in the beginning stages, and she chose the Road Runner to be a part of it. Since it is such a rare car, they had to be careful to get the color and interior correct. She had famed builder Will Posey as the head of the build team. He ensured that it received the correct attention to detail. They also enlisted the team of John Huff, Steve Cutler, and crew out of Casper, Wyoming, to give it the attention that a rare Mopar needs to be correct.

Steve is a detail-oriented Mopar restorer and was able to properly influence the correct finish at the shop in Casper. In September 2021, the completed car was presented to Luke and me at the Muscle Cars at the Mopars at the Strip event.

There are so many wonderful people to thank, but I specifically want to name Phil and Jill Painter, Steve Hinckley, John Huff, Steve Cutler, Courtney Hansen, Bill Sefton, Marco Sandin, Greg Biskey, the Ride of Your Life (ROYL) Garage crew, my wife, my daughter, and Luke for fighting to survive.

We now can enjoy the car to its fullest. We love driving with the top down and setting off car alarms whenever we can. There are still a few things that need to be fixed or modified back to stock original, and we are getting there. I should be able to fix most of it over the winter, and you will find us somewhere in the West on a cruise or at a car show.

Also, a special thanks to Richard Petty for heading to Ford. Without that move, there might have been more than one 1969 Petty Blue Road Runner convertible.

1970 CHEVELLE SS L89/L78

By Rick Nelson

The Chevelle was on top of the world in 1970 with its vaunted 454 LS6. However, it was a much lesser-known engine option that made this SS 396 rarer than any 454-equipped car. (Photo Courtesy Rick Nelson)

General Motors' self-imposed displacement ban on its compact, pony, and midsize models that was instituted in the 1960s is often noted when discussions arise as to why Chevrolet struggled to keep up with Mopar's mighty Hemi throughout the 1960s.

Although it had fully pulled out of factory-supported racing, GM's bread-and-butter manufacturer, Chevrolet, often found ways to circumvent corporate dictations. In some instances, dealers found channels for larger displacement through the central office production orders (COPO). It allowed for fleet orders, and 427s could be installed in 1969 Chevelles and Camaros. Other dealers and outfits simply performed engine swaps at their facilities, such as Baldwin-Motion, the Dick Harrell Performance Center, and Nickey Chevrolet. While all of this took place, Chevrolet found ways to get the most out of its Mark IV 396 engine by offering speed parts.

L89 Aluminum Cylinder Heads

First introduced in 1967 as a cylinder-head option added to the L71 427 Corvette, the L89 was nothing more than a set of aluminum heads installed on the 427 engine. Only 16 L89 Corvettes were produced that year. The heads used on the original 1967 L89 Corvettes were the 3904392 units, and in 1968, the L89 option switched to the 3919842 cylinder head. These heads were slightly revised in late 1969 from the earlier production 842 heads and were only used a short time in production after that. These also used a special head gasket set (3981920). Nothing else on the engine was different, and there was no horsepower improvement. The only change was a 75-pound weight savings.

Because of this, few people ordered the L89 because the only gain was a slight weight savings that came at a very high cost, which in 1969, was $647.50 added to the $252.80 L78 engine option. For comparison's sake and adjusted for inflation, $900.30 in 1969 is equal to $7,068 in 2022, which is a huge cost for an engine option. Production figures for the Camaro and Chevelle were 272 1968 Camaros, 311 1969 Camaros, 400 1969 Chevelles, and 9 1970 Chevelles.

1970 L89s

According to Fran Preve, a well-known GM Tonawanda engine plant historian, a total of only 18 CKT L89 engines were assembled. He went on to state that of the 18, an estimated 9 were slated to be used in the production Chevelles while the other 9 were to be warehoused as warranty or over-the-counter engines. Chevrolet canceled the L89 option early into the model year (November 1969) along with the L78 engine option. Since the aluminum head was never available on the LS6 engine, this November 13–built car is quite possibly the very last L89 production Chevelle produced.

To date, only one 1970 L89 Chevelle has ever surfaced with unquestionable and original documentation as well as complete owner history, which makes this particular Chevelle the only known and documented L89/L78 in the world. Documents consist of the original build sheet that previous owner Brian DeJongh found under the rear seat, Protect-O-Plate, dealer invoice, dealer log book, title transfer history, service records, list of previous owner history, and other paperwork. It is rare to find a lot of documentation on most Chevrolet muscle cars, but to possess this much real documentation on a 1 of 1 car is beyond priceless. To say this is the holy grail of the 1970 Chevelle production or any year of Chevelle is quite the understatement.

Under the valve covers and behind the radiator hose hides the legend-ary L89 aluminum-head option. This Chevelle is the lone surviving 1970 car with that option. (Photo Courtesy Rick Nelson)

Chrome Valve Covers

What makes this story even more unbelievable is that the cylinder-head option was ordered as a mistake by the seller, Virgil Ziebarth of Ziebarth Chevrolet in St. James, Minnesota.

When the original owner, Curt Christensen, entered the dealer-ship in September 1969, he sat down with Ziebarth and placed his order with a specific color and option list within his budget. When he said he wanted the chrome valve covers, which were part of the 396 package anyway, Ziebarth mistakenly checked off the box that noted the L89 Aluminum heads because he thought it was one and the same.

When the car arrived at the dealership on November 25, 1969, all was great—other than the price. Christensen refused to pay for the cylinder-head option, as that was not what he ordered. Between the two, they finally came to an agreement to split the cost. It was a lot of money back in 1969, and it can go down as one of the most valuable mistakes ever made in the muscle-car world.

Ownership History

The car has had a total of six owners to date, which when compared to most muscle cars, is very few. Of those owners, most were the Chevelle's caretakers until the late 1970s and it only changed hands twice since that time.

DeJongh owned the car the longest and was instrumental in locating most of the history of the Chevelle, as well as the documentation, and returned the car to its original glory. In July 2003, after much ground pounding, many phone calls, and other lead tracking, DeJongh connected with Ellis Ziebarth, the Ziebarth dealership owner's son. During a conversation with DeJongh, Ziebarth stated that he still owned all the documentation and dealership memorabilia from 1944 through 1977, and it was housed in a building in St. James, Minnesota.

DeJongh immediately made an appointment with Ziebarth to view and purchase all of the remaining items. It took him a total of three trips to get everything home. DeJongh spent many hours going through the paperwork that he purchased, and he finally found the car's original invoice, Protect-O-Plate, service records, and dealer log

Ellis Ziebarth stands next to the Ziebarth Chevrolet paperwork that showed the L89 option was selected. (Photo Courtesy Rick Nelson)

book. This added to the provenance and value that was already with the car. He also found several NOS dealer items, such as the dealer license-plate frames, which make for a really cool addition to the car.

Restoration

The Chevelle was drag raced both on the street and track in the early 1980s by DeJongh. Its best was a 14.10 quarter-mile ET. The car also gave many years of faithful service and received a couple of basic restorations during its short life that included a color change to black. When the full provenance of the car was discovered in 2003, DeJongh decided to do a full frame-off restoration, so he set out to find all of the parts that he could. He and several of his friends disassembled the car, including the frame, and performed a complete, comprehensive restoration using the skills he had learned from years of working on cars, along with the help of many people.

The restoration was completed in 2010, and DeJongh traveled the show circuit to introduce the extremely rare Chevelle to many enthusiasts. He was rewarded with several wins and a couple of magazine feature articles. In 2013, DeJongh realized that a muscle-car collector needed the car more than he did, and he regretfully sold it.

A muscle-car collector in Florida owned the car until mid-2021 when he also realized the car needed to go to another caretaker. It was sold to a large and prestigious muscle-car collector on the West Coast. During the transport from Florida to the West Coast, the car made a stop at the well-known 1970 Chevelle restoration shop, Muscle Car Restoration and Design. The new owner wanted the shop to do a comprehensive nine-page inspection on the car. During the inspection, several minor issues were found.

The owner received the inspection report, and even though he was very happy with the car overall, there were some items, such as the powder-coated frame and slightly-off gold paint, that he could not live with. He requested that the car be completely torn down and a full no-expense nut-and-bolt restoration be performed. As of this writing, the car is in the final stages of the restoration with hopes of it being the best restored, rarest, and most documented 1970 Chevelle in the world.

1970 FK5 DEEP BURNT ORANGE METALLIC SUPERBIRD
By Alan Munro

The FK5 Deep Burnt Orange metallic is a color that you have to see in person. Seeing it on a Superbird puts this car into its own unique category. (Photo Courtesy Steve Reyes)

In early 1970, Bill Speros Chrysler Plymouth of Memphis, Tennessee, took delivery of a truckload of five 1970 Superbirds. One of those special winged cars turned out to be the rarest of the Superbirds: a factory-painted FK5 Deep Burnt Orange.

In August 1969, Plymouth gave the green light to produce its own outlandish wing car (a close cousin of the prior year's Dodge Daytona) to have a competitive model on the faster NASCAR tracks and attract Richard Petty back to the brand. The challenge was that Plymouth had to make at least 1,920 of them to homologate them. To be fair, they were a bit odd-looking to the general public and pretty pricey for the time. They sold well in some regions of the U.S. but not at all in other areas.

In the Memphis area, Bill Speros did well with selling muscle cars and felt he had a good market for Superbirds. He made a deal with Plymouth to take five more of them, and it was likely a lucrative deal, as Plymouth had a hard time moving the cars. When the truck arrived in Memphis with the five new Superbirds, the fact that one was an FK5 didn't raise any eyebrows at the time.

Superbird History

Much has already been written on the origin of the Plymouth Superbird. Geoff Stunkard's book, *1970 Plymouth Superbird: Muscle Cars in Detail No. 11*, covers this very well and is highly recommended for anyone looking for a greater understanding of these cars' origin, manufacturing, and everything that makes them so coveted by collectors today.

The key points from the Superbird story that are relevant to the origin of our FK5 Superbird is that Plymouth had to produce the required minimum of 1,920 Superbirds by January 1, 1970, for NASCAR to approve them to run that season.

All Superbirds were destined to be built in the massive Lynch Road factory intermixed with various bodystyle Dodge Coronet– and Plymouth Belvedere–based models as they flowed along the assembly line for two days. Since Superbirds require some very special components, the decision was made to use the nearby Clairpointe building to finish, paint, attach the distinctive nose and wing, and add the decals.

The first Plymouth Superbird was completed on October 17, 1969, and the last one left the Clairpointe facility on December 19, 1969. These are key factors in understanding how the FK5 Superbird came to be.

Superbird Colors

Unlike the 1969 Dodge Daytona that was available in all of the 1969 Charger colors, Plymouth went a different route with its new 1970 Superbird. Initially, six colors were offered to dress the NASCAR street machine: EV2 Tor-Red, EK2 Vitamin C Orange, EB5 Blue Fire Metallic, EW1 Alpine White, FY1 Lemon Twist, and FJ5 Limelight. The 999 Corporate (Petty) Blue was added in a subsequent notice to dealers on November 4, 1969.

Why did Plymouth limit the colors? Quite likely to limit the cost. It was estimated that Chrysler had lost over $1,000 on each of the 503 1969 Daytonas produced, and with NASCAR's new rules, Plymouth had to make and sell almost four times as many.

Superbird Marketing

Unlike today, where every announcement from Dodge on the next "Last Call" Challenger special edition is instantly shared and amplified across social media platforms, there was quite a communication lag in the late 1960s.

Since the Superbird was a late production decision, there was no mention of it in the 1970 Belvedere glossy brochure or the special dealership data books to help guide buyers through their purchases. Plymouth created a simple four-page black-and-white document that was sent to all dealers to announce the new model, colors, and features.

The first mass-media publication of the Superbird was in the January 1970 *Motor Trend* magazine, where it scored a cover shot of a Vitamin C Orange Superbird with Dan Gurney sitting atop the rear wing. By the time the magazine hit the newsstands, Superbird production was likely over.

Plymouth only ran two mass-market advertising campaigns for the Superbird. In the February 1970 issue of *Hot Rod* magazine, Plymouth ran a two-page black-and-white ad "announcing a new kind of runner." In April 1970, it followed with ads in several national magazines and featured another two-page black-and-white ad that stated that the Superbird was, "the obvious reason Richard Petty came back." This tied Petty's popularity to the "Win on Sunday, sell on Monday" adage.

In May 1970, *Car and Driver* covered the Daytona 500, where Pete Hamilton won in the Petty Enterprises number 40 Superbird. The reality is, in a pre-internet world, most Superbirds were painted and produced before the muscle-car buyers knew they were coming.

Origin of the FK5 Superbird

Like every good superhero story, this car has its own unique tale. It is important to investigate how this Superbird was made before it arrived at the dealership in Memphis. This question has puzzled many Mopar enthusiasts through the years. There are three theories.

Special Order

In the early factory documentation on the Superbird, there is a NASCAR Master #1 document that outlines a few parameters on the special-order program, initial colors, and has a cryptic notation,

The standard mill on the 1970 Plymouth Superbird was the 440 Super Commando with 375 hp. Optional engines were the 440 6-barrel (390 hp) and the 426 Hemi (425 hp). (Photo Courtesy Steve Reyes)

"Other Colors Available Inquiry #4923." While this sounds like an obvious source of the FK5 Superbird, there are a few problems with that. Research to this date has not found any production documentation that shows more on #4923 or any evidence it was ever used. Two sources going back to the first purchaser and selling dealer do not support that the car was special ordered. There is one troubling anomaly that keeps this theory alive, which is the broadcast sheet that shows this Superbird, RM23U0A177577, is coded Y14 for a sold car. Could it be that someone special ordered the car, the sale did not close, and Bill Speros had it reallocated to his dealership in his bulk buy of five Superbirds? It is a theory.

Production Error, Typo on the Order

Another theory is related to the "QWERTY" keyboard. On the standard typewriter keyboard, the keys for "J" and "K" are beside each other. One theory that is believed to be the most plausible is that a simple typo led to an FK5-paint Superbird being introduced onto the production line.

After enough Superbird-specific parts, such as the V19 special vinyl top, were installed, it was more costly to send it back in an attempt to correct it. There are a few items that support this. Although this FK5 Superbird is the first non-standard paint Superbird to have been identified and publicized, another FK5 4-speed Superbird has been documented in the New York area, and there are rumors of a Hemi car that was ordered in Canada and was possibly lost due to damage or decay. The fact that at least three FK5 Superbirds are alleged (and not a broader spectrum of the Plymouth color pallet) supports the idea that someone made a mistake. Maybe that mistake occurred a few times, as the workers were under pressure to get the Superbird orders in and produced by the deadline.

Production Error, Human Error on the Line

The third theory is regarding another type of production error, where the line workers at the paint department misread the color order on the sheet of "FJ5" as "FK5." The result is similar to the typo theory. Once the Superbird body was painted and the Superbird parts started to go on as it flowed through the massive Lynch Road factory, it was too late to turn it around.

The recently uncovered FE5 Rally Red Superbird might further support this theory. Additional support for the theory of a misread order is the existence of an EB5 Blue Fire Metallic 440+6 Superbird with an original layer of FK5 paint under the blue that was discovered during restoration. In this case, it appears that the error was caught in time for a run back through the paint process. Notably, all these error colors are F color code 5. Maybe it was just that simple: a busy production line and someone read the color code wrong.

The late David J. Patik once interviewed Chrysler Production Engineer Gil Cunningham, who specialized in body sealing and paint at Lynch Road. Gil supported one of the production-error theories. He made specific reference to an FK5 Burnt Orange car that was caught in the trim shop with the vinyl top and a number of other parts installed. The decision was made to send it off to the Clairpointe facility with a can of FK5 paint for the final assembly and out the door in an unintentional color.

RM23U0A177577

This FK5 Superbird was assigned vehicle order number (VON), or job, J98300, which is in the middle of the series that Chrysler assigned to the Superbird production. However, it rolled off the line

The all-important fender tag of the Burnt Orange Superbird denotes color "FK5" on the second line from the bottom (far left). Could the VON on this car (J98300) be an indicator that a batch of special paint colors was set aside to paint toward the end of the model run? (Photo Courtesy Steve Reyes)

as the 1,912th Superbird assembled. It went over to the Clairpointe finishing facility on December 16 ,1970, and left two days later on December 18, 1970, the second to last day of production, with 12 other Superbirds.

Interestingly, the recently discovered FE5 Rally Red Superbird was in the same batch. Some of the other VONs in this last batch have earlier VONs. If other unusual-paint Superbirds surface in future years, it will be interesting to see if they were part of this last batch. That tends to lead credence to an approved special order and late production scheduling to allow for any special finishing paint work.

Owner 1

One day, William and Joyce Knight of Columbus, Mississippi, went car shopping and dropped into Bill Speros Chrysler Plymouth. William saw a dark orange metallic Superbird and had to have it. A deal was struck that included the installation of a Pentastar Chrysler underdash air conditioner to ward off the summer heat and humidity.

The Knights were now the proud owners of a 440 automatic Superbird. William loved the car, and although he drove it a fair bit, he took very good care of it and kept it under the cover of a carport when it was not in use. Unfortunately, the Knights split up in the mid-1970s. Mrs. Knight got the car in the separation, and she decided to sell the Superbird.

Owner 2

Barlow Mann, a young Memphis lawyer, was a real car guy. Although he was still in his 20s and fresh out of law school, he had already owned a series of muscle cars that would make many-a-fan drool today. In a few short years and while going to a university, he had the keys to a variety of cars, including a Z-code 401 AMX Go Pack, a 1 of 6 Buick GS Stage 1 Suncoupe, several 455-powered Oldsmobile 4-4-2 convertibles, a 1968 390 AMX, a Sublime 1970 Challenger T/A, a 1966 Emberglow Mustang 2+2, and a 1970 Shelby GT500 428 SCJ that he received in a trade with his 460 Ranchero GT. That's not to mention the striking Admiralty Blue Metallic over Bright Red interior 1974 Trans Am 455 that he bought new and was able to reacquire many years later. Barlow knew cool muscle cars and was a pretty fair horse trader.

One day in 1977, Barlow looked through the *East Memphis Shoppers News* and saw a rather vague ad for a one-family-owned 1970 Superbird. There were no details, just a phone number. Barlow decided to call and got Joyce Knight. She explained she had gotten the car in the divorce and didn't drive it much, as she didn't like it. She knew that Superbirds were rare (even at that point) and asked a bit more than an experienced car guy like Barlow knew the market would bear. Although he didn't buy it right then and there, they stayed in touch. You don't get involved in as many deals as Barlow had without knowing the power of information in making a good deal.

He visited the local dealer and made friends with the parts manager. He showed Barlow a black-and-white four-page brochure that was sent to the dealers back in 1970 announcing the Superbirds and how they would be great for drawing traffic to their showrooms. In this document, it listed all of the colors the Superbird was offered in and FK5 was not one of them, so Barlow knew the car was rare.

Eventually, in December 1977, Joyce Knight and Barlow Mann came to an agreement for the FK5 Superbird to trade hands for about $3,000. Although the car was in pretty good shape, it had about 50,000 miles on it, had a small ding in the nose, and showed a bit of light wear and tear. He had the small dent repaired and the paint touched up and buffed. He also replaced a molding and a few seals and had it looking as good as new for his weekend driver.

Although the car was seven years old, the Superbird really hauled well for a 440 automatic with all 375 hp still there and ready go at the flex of the right ankle. As a self-professed serial collector, the

Superbird was not destined for a long relationship with Barlow, and in 1978 or 1979, Barlow placed an ad in *Hemmings Motor News* that asked $3,900 for the FK5 oddity.

Owner 3

The ad in *Hemmings* received a lot of attention, and the first person to respond was Carl Hall. Carl was knowledgeable about Superbirds and appreciated that the FK5 color was an anomaly. He and Barlow came to an agreement, and for about $3,600, the rare Superbird was off to its third owner.

Carl wanted the car to be factory stock and removed the dealer air conditioning and installed the front spoiler that had been in the trunk when it was acquired by Barlow. Carl is the first one to really raise the flag in Mopar circles that a unicorn Superbird existed. In the August 1980 issue of the *Winged Warrior* newsletter, there is a note that club member Carl Hall of Centre, Alabama, had a documented FK5 Superbird that the newsletter referred to as the "rarest Superbird." In 1980, the word was getting out in Mopar circles.

Owner 4

In the early 1980s, the Superbird changed hands a couple more times, going to Nebraska, and then to A.J. Poeppe in Wyoming. In the mid-1980s, Dave Jones, a collector from the Indianapolis, Indiana, area got wind of an FK5 Superbird that was for sale in Wyoming through his banker. Dave Jones is no novice collector and is a Mopar guy through and through. He purchased his first Superbird in 1972. Over the course of his life, he has owned more than 200 cars, including 22 of the Mopar aero warriors, 5 of which were factory Hemi cars.

Dave knew a rare wing car when he heard of one, so he reached out to the owner in Wyoming to see if they could make a deal. Initially, the owner changed his mind and wanted to keep the rare 'bird. As he and Dave were communicating, Dave shared a photo of an FF4 Lime Green Metallic AAR that he owned. Poeppe's wife saw the picture and liked that car much better than the winged machine in their driveway, and a deal was made with the AAR and some cash. The FK5 Superbird left Cheyenne and went to its new owner, Dave Jones, in Indiana.

It was during Dave Jones's ownership that the knowledge of this rare Superbird became widely known. Although the sheet metal was all original and in good shape, the car was ready for a refresh, and

Dave had it restored with a fresh paint job to make it probably better than factory new.

In the November 1985 issue of *The Hightailer*, the Daytona-Superbird Auto Club newsletter, Dave made notice of his car in a story titled "A Rare Bird: One of a Kind Superbird." There are a few details that have been clarified over the years, but it was known that it had 60,000 miles at the time and was still the only publicly known Superbird with unusual paint.

Dave announced his plans to show the Superbird in 1986. Although many naysayers were at the shows, Dave had the provenance in the form of the fender tag and broadcast sheet to prove that Mopar produced this FK5 Superbird. Under Dave's stewardship, the nicely freshened FK5 Superbird gained further notoriety, as it was featured in a series of national muscle-car magazines in the late 1980s and early 1990s.

Later Owners

Dave always had some interesting cars in his stable and had thought of selling his FK5 Superbird. He ran an ad in *Mopar Collector's Guide* magazine and received offers over $80,000. Opportunity

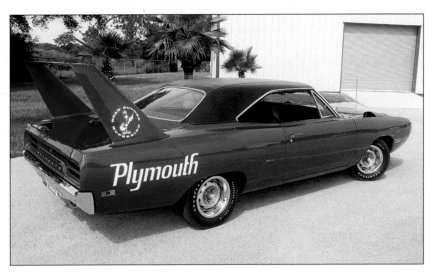

The rear-quarter and wing decals were specially assigned with script black (light-colored cars) and white (dark-colored cars). When this Burnt Orange Superbird came down the line for finishing, someone made the executive decision which color to use, as this color wasn't in the playbook. (Photo Courtesy Steve Reyes)

came knocking in the form of well-known Tampa, Florida, disc jockey Mason Dixon. Mason is a serious Mopar collector and was looking for a wing car, and the Superbird changed hands once again.

Mason enjoyed the car for a year or two, and in an interesting serendipity, Dave and Mason crossed paths while Dave was wintering in Florida. Mason found a 1969 Daytona he wanted, and Dave loved his old rare Superbird, so back into Dave's hands it went. Dave kept it until the mid-1990s when he again made changes in his garage and decided to part company with the rare 'bird for the second time.

Randy Dye, a Stellantis auto dealership owner out of Florida, was living in Huntsville, Alabama, at the time and knew Dave Jones through the hobby. He flew up to Indiana and purchased the Superbird around 1995. Although the Superbird was now 25 years old, it still ran strong, and Randy drove it home from Indiana to Alabama. Randy has had his fair share of interesting Mopars over the years, and after enjoying the Superbird for a while, he decided to sell it in 1997.

Current Caretaker

Fred Menditto had almost bought the rare dark orange Superbird when he heard through his friend Tom Eller that Dave was selling it in 1995. He even went to the Mopar Nationals in Columbus, Ohio, to buy it. However, when the time came, he wasn't ready and picked up a 440+6 Road Runner instead.

A few years later, Tom called to let Fred know that Randy Dye was going to sell it. Knowing that every time it changed hands, the price went up, he decided he better act if he wanted to own this unicorn of a Superbird.

Fred's children were big into junior drag racing and he knew that was going to keep him busy for some years, so he loaned his rare Superbird to the Don Garlits Museum of Drag Racing in Ocala, Florida. It was in residence there from 1999–2020. The museum display highlighted its sticker price of $4,791 and its current value of $250,000.

As of early 2023, the famed "Root Beer Superbird" is back in Fred's personal care. At 53 years old, the FK5 Superbird still has its original sheet metal and about 65,000 miles on it. Fred has no plans to show the car after it was on display for two decades. He will enjoy it personally, drive it sparingly, and take continued good car of this very rare muscle car.

By Mark Sekula

The optional Air Grabber hood was still available for the 1972 Plymouth Road Runner. (Photo Courtesy Arvid Svendsen)

Beginning in early 1969, Chrysler Corporation first offered the 440-ci engine with three 2-barrel carburetors.

The Magnum and Super Commando engine packages debuted exclusively on the midyear Super Bee and Road Runner models, respectively. These cars inherited the nicknames A12 (option code), M-code (440-6 VIN designation), Six Pack (Super Bee), and Six Barrel (Road Runner).

In the spring of 1969, Ronnie Sox wrung out an unreal 12.91 ET at 111 mph at Cecil County Dragway in a tuned Road Runner. Instantly, the 426 Hemi had a viable competitor inside the Mopar engine ranks. People flocked to the dealerships and 3,339 new owners had Mopar's newest hot engine.

The year 1970 proved to be a banner one for the 440-6. The engine was made available on the Challenger R/T, Super Bee, Coronet R/T, 'Cuda, Road Runner, Superbird GTX, and Sport Fury GT. In all,

9,402 tri-carburetor Dodge and Plymouths left the assembly lines. Amazingly, that was 1,502 engines short of the entire 426 Hemi engine run from 1964 to 1971.

A steep dive in production for 1971 saw those numbers dwindle to 1,162 as looming fuel-price increases began to scare away would-be performance-minded buyers.

The 1972 model year saw Chrysler again offer the 440 engine with the three 2-barrel carburetors, but the option fell by the wayside before regular production began. Many have speculated as to why it was canceled. Was it slumping sales? Was the muscle-car era coming to an end because of new U.S. Environmental Protection Agency (EPA) regulations? Was it some other factor? We may never know, but it was likely a combination of all those variables.

For many years, rumors were rampant that a scant few Dodges and Plymouths were produced for the 1972 model year with the 440 Six Pack or Six Barrel option. If one of these beasts survived, it could be proven by the fifth character in the car's serial number. A letter "V" in that location meant that the car was built with this now-unavailable engine.

To date, six of these cars have been identified, and one car is still awaiting discovery.

- WH23V2A100003: Charger
- WH23V2G100006: Charger Rallye (Red)
- WH23V2G100075: Charger Rallye (Yellow)
- RM23V2G100065: RR
- RM23V2G105346: RR GTX (Red)
- RM23V2G111050: RR GTX
- WH23V2A130510: Charger Rallye (Orange)

Performance Car Guide

Magazine scribes were often introduced to some of the coolest muscle cars that would never exist. As manufacturers geared up for another sales year, their newest creations were offered to columnists who wrote for magazines.

In the *Performance Car Guide*'s 1972 issue, in an article titled, "440 Six Pack Road Runner: The Supercar is Dead – Long Live the Road Runner," a tri-carburetor bird was tested. It was geared with a 3.54 Sure-Grip and mated to a 4-speed manual transmission.

Tri-carburation debuted on production models for Dodge and Plymouth in 1969. The Road Runner was the only model to see this setup on four consecutive years of cars. (Photo Courtesy Arvid Svendsen)

Discovery

Amazingly, this 1972 Road Runner GTX (serial number RM23V2G105346) was found in an Effingham, North Carolina, junkyard in the early 1980s. It had been damaged but not beyond repair by today's standards. A Mopar aficionado found the car, saw the letter "V" in its serial number, and knew exactly what it meant. All the rumors of these cars existing created a frenzy of Mopar hunters looking for additional V-code cars. The discoverer was able to purchase the car and save it for future generations to see.

That owner kept the car for about 10 years and collected parts and information about this rare bird. One of the parts he procured was a set of 1972 carburetors that had handwritten tags on them that look to be from Chrysler engineering. It's possibly the only set in existence that were not installed at the factory. Some Chrysler officials he asked refused to acknowledge its existence in public, but when pressed privately, they conceded that a small batch of these cars were produced very early in production. This Road Runner's scheduled production date was August 1, 1971, which was most likely the first day of the 1972-model-year production.

In 1995, the car was sold to a 1972 Road Runner collector in the Chicago area. He spent time collecting a large number of correct and NOS parts for the car but never did any restoration work on the car. That owner did show the car in its unrestored state at the Muscle Car and Corvette Nationals (MCACN) in the Barn Find and Hidden Gems area. The car created an amazing buzz, as only the 440-6 Chargers were public knowledge at the time. A few years later, he sold the car

Like a coyote being neutered, the Road Runner had to cede its 440 engine to the GTX option. Road Runner's largest displacement for its stand-alone model was the 400. This was the GTX's last appearance ever on a Plymouth, and it died with its big-block boots on. (Photo Courtesy Arvid Svendsen)

to its current owners, who had the car restored by Magnum Auto Restoration in LaSalle, Illinois.

Magnum received the car in its derelict state in December 2014 with a goal to have it restored to its original appearance by November 2015 and to be unveiled at MCACN, where it had been shown a few years earlier. That goal was met, and the car now serves as an example of what could have been if the 440 Six Barrel option had continued to be offered.

Sunroof and Other Specifications

The car itself has other notable options. Besides the engine, the most unusual option is the power sunroof. Starting in 1969, Chrysler had a contract with American Sunroof Corporation to take completed vehicles from the factory to its facility and add the sunroof to a finished car. These cars were then shipped to the dealer for sale. The sunroof was considered a factory option available on select cars.

It also has the Air Grabber hood that allowed the driver to move a switch on the dash and the engine vacuum allowed a scoop on the hood to open and let fresh, cold air directly into the carburetors. The radio in the car has both AM and FM bands, but a new-for-1971 option that carried over to 1972 was a console-mounted cassette player. In addition to playing cassette tapes, the driver or passengers could record their voices onto a blank cassette with the attached microphone. It was a truly unique option that was not seen with any other automaker.

The GTX option ended in 1971 as a stand-alone model, but in 1972, it was offered as a package on the Road Runner. It was the only way to get a 440 engine in a Road Runner from 1972 to 1974. That is why you see the GTX emblems on this car in addition to the Road Runner badging.

Was this car destined for a top executive? Was it produced before or after the factory canceled production? Why was the 440 Six Barrel cancelled? We may never know answers to those questions.

What is known is that the 440-6 option didn't survive beyond the early pilot cars. With the 426 vanquished at the end of the 1971 model year, and the cancellation of the 440-6 after these pilot cars, the Mopar muscle-car era began to cruise off into the sunset.

Thankfully, this Road Runner GTX survived to remind us of what could have been.

1972 PONTIAC TRANS AM IN ADRIATIC BLUE

By Ed Dedick

The stunning color of Adriatic Blue was applied to just one 1972 Pontiac Trans Am. Due to a labor strike at GM, only 1,286 T/As traversed the assembly line at Norwood. (Photo Courtesy the American Muscle Car Museum)

The beginning of the apex of the American muscle car was 1969½. A plethora of midyear iron was injected into the marketplace as the manufacturers attempted to squeeze every bit of juice out of their outgoing body platforms.

Road Runners and Super Bees were offered with 440-6 engines. Ford unveiled 428 Cobra Jet Talladegas and Mercury Cyclone Spoilers for homologation purposes. Kenosha, Wisconsin's AMC sent the little Rambler packing with a 390 and a 4-speed (the SC/Rambler).

Pontiac had a few tricks up its sleeves too. The Judge debuted as a package atop the GTO to improve declining year-over-year sales. The big news was a contemporary nameplate on the Firebird platform that carried the performance banner for the next 34 years: Trans Am.

Trans Am

Ideally, the Trans Am nameplate derived from somewhere Pontiac had success. Ford's Talladega won the NASCAR Grand National championship with David Pearson behind the wheel. AMC's SC/Rambler had enough vehicles built to be classified for F/Stock drag racing. The Trans-Am racing series was dominated by Chevrolet and Ford. In fact, a Trans Am car never competed in a Trans-Am race in 1969. That honor went to its stablemate, the Firebird.

The Trans Am capitalized on styling, flair, and performance. The limited production numbers for 1969 (697 units) peaked in 1979 when *Smokey and the Bandit* influenced sales of 117,108. However, it was slow going for the first three years.

Norwood

Starting in 1972, GM's Norwood, Ohio, plant was the sole producer of the F-body Camaros and Trans Ams. Only 1,286 Trans Ams were made for 1972 due to a 174-day labor strike at the Norwood, Ohio, GM plant that began on April 8, 1972. This strike was between the United Auto Workers (Local 674) and plant management. It was finally resolved on September 7, 1972. This was an interesting year for GM, with the 174-day strike severely limiting production. The normal production schedule was generally 48 weeks out of the model year. With work stoppages and equipment setup being limited, production was reduced to 22 weeks for the 1972 model year.

Federal Safety Standards

Unfortunately, the timing of the strike meant that cars produced after September 1, 1972, had to meet the federally mandated 1973 safety front-impact bumper regulations. When the UAW workers returned, there was too much work to be done in order to produce cars again. Imagine trying to start again after five months of not producing a single car.

A few Firebird models that were in their final stages of assembly were completed and sold as 1972 models. GM had no choice but to crush and scrap 1,100 cars that remained in various stages of assembly that did not comply with the new 1973 bumper-impact standards. On a positive note, 40 of the cars were stripped of their VINs and donated to local trade schools.

Special-Color Trans Ams

Pontiac had a firm stance, starting in the early 1970s, on having only two exterior colors for the Trans Am models: code 11 Cameo White and code 26 Lucerne Blue. This was the case until 1972, when a handful of special colors were produced. From November 1971 to late March 1972, a total of five cars received special paint: two cars in Starlight Black, one in Cardinal Red, one in Revere Silver, and the Adriatic Blue car featured here.

My Story

This Trans Am has "DD" listed on the invoice and "24-24" (Code 24) stamped on its data tag. It also has a factory-commissioned Brass Hat concept special interior of ivory and blue with blue seat belts, which are documented with handwritten marks on the build sheet. Adriatic Blue later became an optional factory Trans Am color in 1974.

This car was built during the week of March 22–28, 1972, at the Norwood plant. It was redirected from the target dealership Friendly Pontiac-GMC in Temple, Texas, to Pete Ganis Pontiac in Fort Worth, Texas. Pete drove the car for a year as a demonstrator, and this is likely where the car lost some of its provenance as a rare 1of 1.

Unknown days of hot rodding and street racing finally led to the

An ivory interior paired beautifully with the white exterior stripe and shaker hood. Ivory and blue seat belts topped off the color combination. (Photo Courtesy the American Muscle Car Museum)

car being used in the late 1970s in East Texas pastures to herd dairy cows back into the barns. The original front bumper had scratch marks from the fields and cows, and this is likely where the front spoilers were torn off.

Hiding in plain sight on the side of Texas State Highway 69 in the mid-1980s, this car was visited by many Pontiac enthusiasts. At the time, most believed this car was not a real Trans Am with the non-standard exterior and interior colors and the code 24-24 trim tag. The car fell into poor shape after years of neglect.

The car was purchased by an unknown person who hauled it to Houston, Texas. He removed the engine, transmission, and rear axle and placed the parts for sale on eBay. The winning bid was from noted Pontiac restorer Steve Schappaugh from Lincoln, Nebraska. Steve arrived to pick up the Trans Am drivetrain and inquired about the body. The seller thought it was a Firebird and intended to scrap the body. Steve struck a deal and brought home the whole car.

Once the car made it to Steve's shop, longtime customer and friend Greg San Marco of San Antonio, Texas, purchased the car and had Steve's shop, Muscle Car Memories, perform a full professional rotisserie restoration. Greg was so enthused about the car that he gave it the nickname *Adrian* and made it a matching-colors cake on its birthday. In July 2015, Greg sold this special car to Mark Pieloch.

The Restoration

Meticulous attention to detail was given to this car. Fine details from the correct copper-coated cotter pins on the steering linkage to pink and yellow paint dobs on the steering knuckle set this restoration apart from others. It has the blue/white/orange paint dobs on the rear axle to the correct red oxide underbody color with paint oversprays and paint undersprays. This special Trans Am has all the original sheet metal and retains its numbers-matching LS5 455 H.O. V-8 engine and the M-22 4-speed transmission.

Adrian had never been shown before, and once the restoration was completed in the fall of 2014, it was unveiled at the 2014 MCACN show. The car won the concourse-level Gold Award and scored 978 of a possible 1,000 points. At the same event, it was chosen by automotive car artist Michael Irvin for the Sponsor's Pick Award. This car went on to the Good Guys Lone Star Nationals and was a top-five Muscle Car of the Year finalist, won the Concourse d'Elegance of

Topping off the Trans Am's 455 H.O. engine is a shaker air cleaner. (Photo Courtesy the American Muscle Car Museum)

Texas 2015 Best of Class award, and was chosen for the PPG Platinum distributor 2016 calendar.

    Adrian is still owned by Mark Pieloch. He is the owner and founder of the American Muscle Car Museum, located in Melbourne, Florida, where the car is on display for thousands to enjoy every year. It receives continuous maintenance by the experienced staff at the museum.

Pete Ganis Pontiac in Fort Worth, Texas, received this Trans Am in 1972. Ganis drove the car for a year as a demonstrator. (Photo Courtesy the American Muscle Car Museum)

CHAPTER 3

Super-Car Tuners and Builders

"Anything you can do, I can do better." These are the cars that are sometimes viewed as being a cut above their factory production counterparts.

In the world of the muscle car, it's the super car that slams the auction gavel down the hardest. Whether it's a Yenko Camaro, Tasca Mustang, or a Mr. Norm's supercharged Demon, the personal touches that these legends put on a vehicle ices the muscle-car cake.

For many, these creations are fairly recognizable and known. However, each of these builders also created muscle cars that have remained off the public's radar—and it wasn't just builders. Zone managers, regional managers, dealerships, racers, and promoters all had a hand in creating this unique genre. Some were designed to be available to the masses and built in as many or as few as could be sold, while some were singularly built for promotions. Either way, each of these cars are a crown jewel in many collections.

1965 FORD TASCA 505 MUSTANG

By Wes Eisenschenk

Bob Tasca (right) was no stranger to the walls of Ford Motor Company. He was one of Ford's highest-volume sellers of automobiles. Here, he receives the coveted Perfect Performance Car of the Year award from American Rodding *Executive Editor Lyle K. Engel. (Photo Courtesy Bob Tasca Family Archives)*

If Ford Motor Company was to stick a feather in its cap regarding a single automobile dealership that perpetuated high-performance, that feather would be Tasca Ford.

In 1962, Gordon Carlson purchased a new 1962 Galaxie 406-ci/405 from Tasca Ford. Gordon's family had been long-time customers of Tasca, and the Ford Galaxie wasn't cutting the mustard against the souped-up Chevrolets, Pontiacs, Dodges, and Plymouths in the local races. One day, while he had the Galaxie in for mechanical work, Gordon mentioned he could use a new set of tires so that he could be competitive against the GMs and Mopars that had been giving him fits.

Tasca gathered some employees and had a group discussion about what could be done to help Gordon. Sensing a trend in the market and an opportunity to grow the Tasca brand, Gordon bought a new set of tires, and Bob Tasca sent out an order for high-performance FE engine parts. Tasca-sponsored drag racing was off and running.

The newly formed Tasca Racing Team succeeded early and won trophies at the Charleston drag strip, but Gordon was hesitant to go full-tilt with his street/strip car and committed the Galaxie to strip-only performance. Bob decided to end the partnership and run his own car.

Throughout the 1960s, Tasca dominated the world of drag racing. Gear-jammer Bill Lawton became a household name from campaigning Galaxies, Fairlanes, and Mustangs. Other racers who ran under Tasca sponsorship included Bobby Price, Hubert Platt, and Mario Andretti.

Personalized Cars and the Alexander Brothers

Bill Lawton brought notoriety to Tasca via the drag strip, so Bob Tasca looked internally to bring street-oriented, performance-minded individuals into the dealership.

Bob set about to create 20 personalized cars in the mid-1960s to fulfill that objective. With help from the Alexander Brothers (Mike and Larry) from Detroit, Michigan, Bob envisioned classy-yet-bone-jarring hot rods to boost the image of Tasca Ford and capture the imagination of would-be customers who wanted customization work.

By the mid-1950s, the "A Brothers" were well-known in the Detroit area for custom work on their own cars and for those of friends and acquaintances. By the late 1950s, they made a concentrated effort to have their customs featured but received negative feedback on the lighting and composition of their photos. After an encounter at their shop with George Barris via Promotions Inc. co-president Bob Larivee, the A Brothers utilized Barris's influence with the magazines, and their cars started to get featured. After that, their clientele list grew exponentially.

Tasca Bird-1 and Fairlane TGT

A pair of cars Bob created received a fair amount of national recognition. The Tasca Bird-1 featured a blueprinted 427 medium-riser engine that was allegedly installed on the assembly line at Ford Motor

The Tasca Bird-1 was fitted with a 427 engine at the factory with Bob Tasca's insistence. From there, it was driven back to Tasca Ford for some further engine detailing and tuning by John Healy. (Photo Courtesy Bob Tasca Family Archives)

Company. A Cruise-O-Matic auto transmission was paired behind the 427. The Bird-1 wore Cibie rectangular headlights, a staple of customizers, with 26 coats of Candy Red paint and a bar-tube grille. The lowered machine sported reshaped fenders and a reshaped hood and featured a unique set of Tasca 427 emblems. The car was dressed with Lincoln MKII turbine wheel covers that sat atop thin-stripe whitewall tires. Tasca claimed 0-60 in 6 seconds with a top speed around 135 mph.

The Fairlane was another 427-transplant Alexander Brothers creation. A stock 1966 Fairlane GTA was customized by the A Brothers

Another of the famous Tasca Ford creations was the Fairlane TGT. It also received customization from the Alexander Brothers and the vaunted Ford 427. (Photo Courtesy Bob Tasca Family Archives)

and featured extended fenders and horizontally stacked Cibie head-lights. In true fashion, the brothers loaded the Fairlane with pounds of beautifully deep Kelly Green metalflake paint. The Fairlane was de-badged on the exterior.

The 427 FE powerplant retained Ford's C-6 automatic transmission and received grip through a 3.91:1 Traction Lok differential in a 9-inch housing. A 780-cfm Holley 4-barrel carburetor sat atop the FE.

Both the Tasca Bird-1 and Fairlane TGT remain unaccounted for.

Tasca 505 Mustang

As fantastic as the Tasca Bird-1 and Fairlane TGT creations turned out to be, they were overshadowed by the cover-worthy Tasca 505 Mustang. The runaway sales success that was the Ford Mustang didn't stop customizers from taking something great and making it perfect, and that's exactly what Bob Tasca did.

As amazing and cutting edge as the 1965 Ford Mustang Fastback platform was, Bob Tasca found a way to make it even better. Once again, the Alexander Brothers massaged their magic into the creation. Bob called them the "Michelangelos of the automotive business" in the December 1965 issue of *American Rodding: The Magazine of Performance Cars*.

Cibie headlights filled the front fenders, and the front-fascia park-ing lights were recessed behind the customized front grille that fea-tured nine horizontal bars. Ford's running-horse grille emblem was removed and replaced with an emblem that was offset to the driver's side. A pair of rectangular callouts were fastened to the fenders featur-ing "Tasca," a centered flag, and "505" positioned inside the badging.

Shelby side scoops were grafted behind the doors, but they were non-functional, as they did not aid in brake cooling. The power front-wheel disc brakes were paired with a pressure proportioning valve between the front discs and rear drums to keep brake-line pressure from getting too high during a hurried stop.

The rear bumper was cut and formed into the rear panel of the car, which had been extended 2.5 inches with a recessed decklid. The gas cap was moved into the trunk, and T-bird sequential taillights were recessed behind a matching set of horizontal bars to cap off the tail. Topping off the aesthetics were three racing stripes (two thin and one thick) that traversed the length of the Mustang from stem to stern atop 25 coats of Pearlescent White lacquer.

What about the 505?

To achieve this gaudy horsepower rating, Bob had the guys at the shop stretch the 289 out to 325 ci and use a 3/8-inch stroker crank. The heads featured new combustion chambers that had 1.96-inch intake valves and 1.625-inch exhaust valves. The compression ratio was 11.34. Shelby's all-aluminum transmission shifted the powerplant to shed 45 pounds off the gross weight and sent the power back to a set of 3.89:1 gears. Two Holley carburetors sat atop the high-rise manifold.

The inside of the 505 sported a Persian rug carpet, LTD courtesy lights, stereo reverberation, and simulated wood-grain. The seats featured Mustang logos that were embossed onto the leather. Hurst 6-inch wheels rode on one-off Goodyear Double Eagle rubber. Weight-saving measures were taken at every opportunity.

Tasca claimed low-12-second quarter-mile times with a top end in the 145-plus-mph range.

American Rodding had seen and felt enough with the Tasca 505 and crowned the car with its "Perfect Performance Car" title for the 1965 model year. Tasca took the car to one of Ford's divisional headquarters where Ford Vice President Donald Frey and Bob Tasca received the award and silver bowl from *American Rodding* Executive Editor Lyle Engel.

Legacy

After receiving its adulation, the 505 Mustang sat on the showroom at Tasca Ford, where it was roped off and had flowers positioned around the glistening silver bowl. A pair of hood scoops were added to cap off the build.

After a couple years of carrying the Tasca creativity banner, the 505 was sold to a private party who found it on the lot at Paul Harvey Ford in Indianapolis, Indiana.

After being off the grid for decades, the Tasca 505 Mustang returned to the spotlight in 2007 when it appeared in a Mustang club magazine. Some custom striping was added to the side of the car, but other than that, the Tasca 505 remained unscathed. At the time of this writing, the car is privately owned, but rest assured, Bob Tasca's mightiest small-block creation is still one of the showiest feathers in his hall of fame hat.

1966 SHELBY 427 COBRAS (THE COBRA "SUPER SNAKES" TWIN-PAXTON SUPERCHARGED)

By Colin Comer

The CSX 3015 is quite possibly the most menacing muscle car ever produced. Adorned in Guardsman Blue with its Super Snake hood, it sold for a record haul of $5.5 million at Barrett-Jackson in 2007. (Photo Courtesy Barrett-Jackson)

Shelby American employees were junkies—horsepower junkies, that is. Carroll Shelby had a knack for routinely egging them on to see what kind of machines they were capable of building. Remember, this was a shop chock full of red-blooded California hot rodders who knew how to make stuff go really fast. In 1967, Carroll Shelby's 427 Cobra reportedly was no match above 140 mph for his friend and former attorney Stan Mullin's Ferrari 275 GTB/4 during their driving competition on weekend trips to Lake Tahoe on Route 395. The big Texan laid out the marching orders to his crew: build a Cobra that Stan's Ferrari couldn't whoop.

The result was the first twin-Paxton 427 Cobra.

CSX 3015

Using CSX 3015, a 427 competition-spec car that was originally used as a Ford public relations car in England, as its starting point, the crew at Shelby American decided that the 427 needed forced induction to cope with its brick-like aerodynamics and the higher altitude of the run to Tahoe. The only thing better than one Shelby/Paxton supercharger was two Shelby/Paxton superchargers. It was the proverbial 10 pounds of stuff in a 5-pound bag, but this crew found a way to make it work.

To hedge a bet before the Paxtons went on, the crew built a 427 side-oiler engine with aluminum medium-rise heads and a Mickey Thompson cross-ram intake. The superchargers fed boost through two pressurized bonnets, one mounted atop each Holley 4-barrel carburetor. Of course, with all this hardware on top of the 427, an already-cramped engine bay literally overflowed with machinery, so a somewhat ridiculous hood scoop was fitted to clear it all. It was functional but certainly not complimentary to the voluptuous lines of the Cobra. Picture your favorite supermodel with a world-class beer belly, and you get the idea. In the end, despite its unfortunate hood bulge, the bright blue 427 Cobra had a menacing appearance.

With an estimated output in the 800-hp range and an insane amount of torque, the crew thought that there wasn't a clutch or a 4-speed transmission that could survive behind it. As a result, a special Ford Cruise-O-Matic 3-speed automatic transmission transmitted this prodigious power to a 3.31:1 rear differential. With all of that torque, there was no need for steeper gearing. Remember, this thing had to be capable of showing its taillights to a Ferrari on the big end. God forbid that ol' Shel ran out of RPM anywhere south of where that damn Ferrari did.

Needless to say, the twin-Paxton car was a weapon, and the Cobra easily won the next match between Shelby and Mullin.

"That darn thing literally [sic] exploded past 140 mph," Mullin said. "It ate my Ferrari alive!"

Shelby was reported to have driven the CSX 3015 in this configuration on a few high-speed runs. Reportedly, he was clocked at 190 mph. On another run, the massive supercharger belt was thrown off at high RPM, stranding the car. Another high-speed run led to the death of a buzzard on the Cobra's windshield.

In February 1968, *Road & Track* magazine called the 3015 "The Cobra to End All Cobras."

In the end, all who drove the 3015 were praying for safety because it was not a very controllable vehicle by all accounts. Any sane person in Shelby's shoes would think that the point was made and there was no need to duplicate the evil that was his personal twin-Paxton supercharged 427 Cobra, but no one said Shelby was sane when it came to horsepower or automotive excess.

CSX 3303

In June 1967, during a discussion about cars between Shelby and his friend, the now-disgraced Bill Cosby, the comedian bragged to Shelby about his new Ferrari, which led to Shelby's offer to build Cosby a 200-mph Cobra that could "kick any Ferrari's ass." Cosby was understandably intrigued. In 1967, 200 mph was a speed only seen on the Bonneville Salt Flats and not in a production road car. Cosby accepted the challenge, and Shelby had another blue 427 Cobra PR car, a street-specification one in this case, modified to the same twin-supercharged configuration as his CSX 3015.

Shortly thereafter, the CSX 3303 was delivered to Cosby at his home. His experience driving the car was relayed in a 24-minute stand-up comedy routine that became the title track of his album, which was fittingly titled "200 M.P.H." It seems that Cosby didn't make it out of his yard without being scared to death of his twin-Paxton car,

One-time funny man Bill Cosby noted that Carroll Shelby approached him about driving foreign cars. He told Cosby, "You're an American, right? Drive an American car." So, Cosby tasked him with building a car that could go more than 200 mph. Carroll obliged.

largely because of a sticky throttle. It is reported that Cosby drove it less than half of a mile in total.

Cosby gave this car to the wife of his manager. She drove it for a few months, and when she became pregnant, the car was returned to Shelby American by her husband, who feared for the well-being of their unborn child.

The 3303 was eventually sold to S&C Motors of San Francisco in April 1968. It was later sold to Tony Maxey, who was stopped by the California Highway Patrol and given a speeding citation during the second weekend he had the car. After he received the ticket, Maxey started the car, the throttle stuck, and he immediately lost control of the car and careened down a steep embankment toward Lake Berryessa. Maxey was thrown from the car and mortally wounded, as was the Cobra. It was reported that Maxey died from his injuries in the week following the horrific crash.

"Super Snake"

What about the name "Super Snake?" Originally used as the official name of an earlier, special-427-powered 1967 GT500, the term is often used to refer to these two twin-Paxton supercharged Cobras. It came about in 1968 when Al Dowd of Shelby American placed an ad to sell the CSX 3015 and referred to it as Carroll Shelby's Personal Super Snake. Officially, the crew who built these cars at Shelby American simply called them the twin-Paxton cars. It was short and sweet.

Did They Survive?

Where are these two twin-Paxton cars today? The CSX 3015 was eventually sold in 1970 to musician and songwriter Jimmy Webb, who penned dozens of hit songs for Glen Campbell in the 1960s and 1970s. Webb held on to the 3015, despite, in his own words from 1991, having to "defend this car tooth and nail against accountants, wives, and girlfriends for almost 20 years."

That worked until the Internal Revenue Service (IRS) proved to be too worthy of an opponent and took everything Webb had in 1995. It was sold by the IRS at auction and went through a few owners before it became the feature car at the Barrett-Jackson Scottsdale auction in January 2007. It sold for an astounding world-record price of $5.5 million to collector Ron Pratte. In January 2015, Pratte sold the

CSX 3015 at Barrett-Jackson for $5,115,000. In 2021, the car slithered across the Barrett-Jackson stage for a third time, where it sold for $5.5 million.

The CSX 3303 has led an interesting life. Well, let's call it an after-life. The 3303 was resurrected from the dead and is still with us today. Originally an organ donor, the 3303's engine and suspension were used as the basis for a 1923 Ford hot rod in the mid-1970s. The serial number and rights to it ended up in England, where they were affixed to a new chassis and body (now right-hand drive) that assumed the identity of the CSX 3303. The original engine was later found and reunited with the other various bits that are now known as the 3303, and the car was restored to its original left-hand-drive twin-Paxton configuration.

While many think you can never have enough power, the twin-Paxton 427 Cobra Super Snakes may be proof that there is a limit. They stand as the high-horsepower champions of the Cobra world, yet those who have been brave enough to pilot one all agree they are too damn much. But for guys like Carroll Shelby, who wanted to make sure that his legal counsel wasn't faster than he was, too much seemed to be just enough.

A 1965 427 side-oiler with aluminum medium-riser heads and a Mickey Thompson cross-ram intake sat below the two Paxton superchargers. The output was in the 800-hp range. (Photo Courtesy Barrett-Jackson)

1967 CHEVROLET GORRIES BLACK PANTHER CAMARO

By Duncan Brown

One of the most unique and handsome offerings was the 1967 Black Panther Camaro. Gorries Downtown Chevrolet Oldsmobile put together this program out of Toronto, Ontario, Canada. (Photo Courtesy David Newhardt/Mecum Auctions)

The September 29, 1966, release of the 1967 Chevrolet Camaro was aimed at the same market as the Ford Mustang. Both cars shared a similar wheelbase and short-rear-deck and long-hood design. The Camaro's wider stance provided curvier looks and better handling. The Camaro originally offered only two V-8s: a 327 and a Camaro-exclusive 350 for the Super Sport (SS) option.

Ford widened the 1967 Mustang's stance and engine bay with a 390 engine option to trump the Camaro. While Chevrolet scrambled to coordinate official 396 engine options for the Camaro, independent builders and dealerships swapped in 396s and 427s. Many of these specialists offered unique appearance modifications as well.

Panthers, Cougars, and Tigers

In Toronto, Ontario, Canada, in the fall of 1966, Gorries Downtown Chevrolet Oldsmobile created a specialty Camaro package called the Black Panther. Chevrolet Motor Division originally toyed with the name "Panther" when it named the new Camaro. The September 30, 1966, debut of the 1967 Mercury Cougar contributed to Chevrolet's decision to relinquish the Panther name—but there was more to it.

The primary cause for the demise of the aggressive Panther name stemmed from GM's need to downplay bad press from Ralph Nader's safety crusade and government threats of an antitrust case. GM further assuaged its critics by moving on from Pontiac Motor Division's highly evocative tiger marketing theme in late 1966.

Gorries Performance Promotion

Unlike GM, Gorries made its mark through unrestrained performance promotion. Gorries was established by A.D. Gorrie in 1917 as a Ford dealership. When Joseph L. Seitz bought Gorries, he retained the well-recognized name. Gorries experienced a few franchise switches by the time Joseph's grandson Ernest Burke Seitz, known as Burke, joined the dealership. Burke was born on January 23, 1925. After serving as a Royal Canadian Air Force pilot in World War II, Burke transformed Gorries into a hive of racing activity in the 1950s.

Burke personally drove in races and sponsored numerous drivers in rallies, road racing, and drag racing. Burke's expert race preparation mechanics handled Gorries customer performance tunes, engine swaps, and hop-ups. Gorries muscle-car salesman Jerry Coffey was born on January 18, 1924. At 30 years old, Jerry was reported to be the highest-volume Corvette salesman in Canada.

The Gorries team envisioned a great-looking specialty Camaro with flexible levels of performance and luxury. The majority of Black Panthers were built as a solid starting point with escalating levels of performance, depending on the purchaser's budget.

Two Z/28s became promotional Black Panthers. Craig Fisher raced one in the Trans-Am series. A 396-ci, 360-hp Black Panther with a 4-speed transmission, Positraction, disc brakes, Corvette side pipes, and the quick-steering option became the official pace car at Mosport International Raceway in Ontario, Canada.

Customer Black Panthers

Customer Black Panthers included a convertible and several Rally Sport (RS) and SS models, but Gorries focused primarily on base Camaro

The perfectly-at-home 327 provided 210 hp. The Chevrolet-orange engine contrasted greatly with the black paint of the Black Panther Camaro. (Photo Courtesy David Newhardt/Mecum Auctions)

sport coupes. Most Black Panthers relied on the 327-ci, 210-hp engine that was an oversquare rev-happy motor and unencumbered with smog equipment. A fairly even mix of automatic or 4-speed manual transmission Black Panthers were produced.

Although an early Black Panther was a Sierra Fawn car that was repainted black, Gorries usually ordered a Tuxedo Black 1967 Camaro to start. It typically included the Z21 option with a chrome roof drip gutter and wheel arch moldings. The Gorries body shop painted a front gold bumblebee wraparound stripe in the approximate location that Chevrolet RS and SS stripes were normally applied. A gap in the stripes on each front fender left space for Black Panther nameplates that appeared on the rear decklid and inside console. A body-length gold stripe was added above the rocker panel. A gold pinstripe emphasized the bodyline crease.

Most Black Panthers had a gold interior and the Z87 option, which added chrome spokes on the steering wheel, full-length molded armrests on the doors, a glove-box light, and trunk mat. The Z23 option added bright pedal and A-pillar trim.

007 Panel

Many Black Panthers were equipped with Gorries optional "007" panel. Between the bucket seats, the flip-up console concealed

The tongue-in-cheek gauges were reminiscent of the 007 movie cars from the 1960s. The only thing missing was James Bond. (Photo Courtesy David Newhardt/Mecum Auctions)

dummy toggle switches that were labeled "Ejection Seat," "Bullet Shield," "Oil slick," etc. These switches mimicked the control panel in the Aston Martin used by the character James Bond in the films *Goldfinger* and *Thunderball*.

Panthers and Tiger Paws

The factory 14x5-inch steel wheels and D78 (7.35-inch) tires were replaced on Black Panthers with 14x6-inch Magnum 500 mag wheels with 8.55-inch red-stripe U.S. Royal Tiger Paw tires. In 1967, U.S. Royal changed its name to Uniroyal.

Beginning in October 1963, U.S. Royal Super Safety 880 XP redline tires were standard equipment on the Pontiac GTO. The 880 XPs were rechristened as "Tiger Paws" in 1964 to augment Pontiac's Tiger marketing. U.S. Royal tests proclaimed that Tiger Paws accelerated, cornered, and stopped better than other tires and could run for 100 miles at 120 mph or 17,000 miles at 83 mph without failure.

With a responsive 327-ci engine in a lightweight Camaro with improved Tiger Paw handling, the basic Black Panther was a great looking, competent platform. Gorries speed department could progressively develop the car with headers, cam, ignition, and suspension upgrades.

Gorries Performance Manager George Moss drove a Black Panther SS 396 demonstrator with a 427 short-block substitution. Moss's car had a black interior with a factory wood wheel and console gauges. In May 1967, *Canada Track & Traffic* ran Moss's demonstrator from 0 to 60 mph in 6.8 seconds on a wet road. The 427-ci, 435-hp engine teamed with a 4-speed transmission and 4.10:1 axle. Front disc brakes and higher spring and shock rates made the beast manageable.

Franchise Sales

Gorries franchised Black Panthers in Ontario, Canada, to Myers Motors Co. in Ottawa, Eastown Chevrolet Oldsmobile Ltd. in London, and Webster Motors Ltd. in Windsor. Terry McLean, a Webster's performance salesman, built at least four Black Panthers on site following the Gorries template. A Webster Panther received the L30 327-ci, 275-hp engine paired with a 4-speed transmission. Beginning in mid-1967, this combination triggered the factory installation of parts that were commonly thought to be exclusive to SS Camaros, such as the rear radius rod and 12-bolt rear. These sleepers are SS-tinged 327s.

Chevrolet Motor Sales Ltd. in Montreal, Quebec, Canada, and Bob Johnson Chevrolet in Halifax, Nova Scotia, Canada, also stocked the Panthers. A dealership all the way down in New Orleans, Louisiana, also reportedly carried the Panthers.

The general consensus is that fewer than 50 Black Panthers were produced. Headlines that featured shootouts between the police and Black Panther activists in the U.S. politicized the Black Panther Camaro name. The Black Panther Camaros were already fading out because the Gorries building was sold. The staff's energy was focused on consolidating into Burke's other high-performance dealership: Golden Mile Motors Ltd. in Scarborough, Ontario, Canada.

One intriguing 1968 Camaro has surfaced that may have been a late candidate for conversion. Vintage Vehicles Canada confirmed that it was ordered by Gorries in Tuxedo Black with a gold interior.

Panther Survivors

The 1967 Black Panther Camaros could regularly be found as used cars for sale in Ontario until 1972, after which they appeared infrequently. Some dealer-special runs of 50 cars have left no survivors (the 1970 Pontiac Magnum 400) or just one (the 1970 Pontiac LeMans Jury).

A "Black PAN-THER" decal was placed above the automatic shifter on the center console. The gold carpeting paired well with the exterior gold accents. (Photo Courtesy David Newhardt/ Mecum Auctions)

Currently, the one Black Panther known and verified in the collector hobby was owned by Bob Simonen of Sault Ste. Marie, Ontario, Canada. Bob was born on December 6, 1940. He was 26 years old when he paid Gorries $3,625 for a 327-ci automatic Black Panther on April 7, 1967. Bob owned it until his death on July 5, 2018. Bob's Panther was auctioned by Mecum, and Mecum's research concluded that it was 1 of 1.

Contenders exist, but the collector hobby can only evaluate known cars. Some people prefer to maintain their privacy, which can result in legitimate cars being overlooked. However, sometimes when rumored cars are finally tracked down, they turn out to be tributes or clones. At this point, no one can say for sure, but there are two more strong contenders for authenticity.

It has been reported that a man named Doug who lives somewhere north of Toronto bought a 327-ci, 275-hp, 4-speed Black Panther RS from Gorries in December 1966 with the rarely seen headrest option and console gauges. The original 327 engine is long gone and was replaced with a 396, but word is that the body is original.

A man named Shawn purchased an 89,000-mile 1967 Camaro that had been repainted. It is believed to have been bought new from Gorries by Patrick Newbound in 1967 as a Black Panther with the 007 console. Shawn purchased the car from the son of the original owner. In both these cases, there is a strong possibility that original paperwork may exist to verify the cars. For now, Bob Simonen's car is 1 of 1 and likely the only original body and drivetrain example that is known.

1968 AMC AMX VON PIRANHA

By Wes Eisenschenk

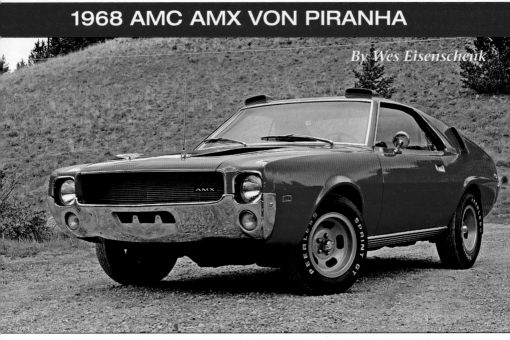

A handful of AMC dealerships and zones took on the task of creating customized, warrantied cars. Few AMCs were this flamboyant. (Photo Courtesy Scott Lachenauer)

B y now, most of us have read about various one-off AMCs that were created by a zone, district, or dealership with the intention to drive customers onto showroom floors. Perhaps the most known of these were the Randall AMC Gremlins that had a 401 engine shoehorned into the engine bay. Wisconsin had the Badger Javelin, which was a dress-up package on the 1969-model-year car that featured a drive-away promotion that marked AMC's 15th anniversary in Milwaukee. Each Javelin was Frost White and had a red C-stripe accompanied by a red interior. Production numbers sit at 80 total units.

But, how many of you are familiar with a South American fish that had its name applied to AMC's newest two-seater hot rod, sharply named the Von Piranha AMX?

It would be rewarding to lay out a similar story to those that you've heard so many times with dealerships and regional specials, such as the Yenko Super Cars or the Twister Special Mustangs. Unfortunately, that's not possible with the Von Piranhas. The information about them is scarce, so let's unveil what we do know and see if this story can shake loose more information on the 1968 Von Piranha AMXs.

Thoroughbred Motors

Clarel Stark Trosper created Thoroughbred Motors in Oklahoma City, Oklahoma, which had its grand opening on November 12, 1955. As a racer himself, Clarel fancied exotic cars and stocked his dealership with vehicles from Mercedes-Benz, Jaguar, and Austin-Healey. In October 1962, things went south when Trosper was indicted on 19 counts regarding false corporate tax returns from 1956, 1957, and 1958 and was sentenced to five months in a federal prison.

After serving his time, Trosper moved west and opened another dealership in September 1965. Trosper, who now went by C.S. Trosper, began to expand his business and created Thoroughbred Car Co. at 2353 E. Highway 24 in Colorado Springs, Colorado. He continued to stretch the Thoroughbred franchise two years later and added a location in Tucson, Arizona. A third spot, named Thoroughbred Motor Co., opened in Englewood, Colorado, in late 1967, and specialized in the second-most-imported car into the U.S.: the Datsun.

Von Piranha

As of this writing, only two confirmed examples have been accounted for: the car featured here and another AMX that sold on Craigslist in 2019. Both cars were Matador Red with a red interior. The Craigslist car was painted gold at one point but retained its original color in the engine bay and doorjambs.

Here's where we start wading into the weeds a bit. The creation of the Von Piranha is thought to have originated at Thoroughbred Motors at either the Colorado Springs or Denver location. A few publicity photos were generated and circulated showing Denver roadracer Ron Hunter behind the wheel of a Von Piranha at Continental Divide Raceway in Castle Rock, Colorado, possibly circa 1968. Hunter's Von Piranha is red and could be one of the two surviving cars. There's also rumors of a blue Von Piranha in the Denver area that still frequents car shows.

So, what did a Von Piranha entail? We can only go by what exists on the two surviving cars and word of mouth. For starters, the Von Piranha had four scoops: two on the roof and two on the sail panels. The C-panel scoops were functional and aided in cooling the brakes. The roof scoops were bug catchers. Rumors suggest they may have been functional on other Von Piranhas and served as a forced

Roof scoops? Well, yeah. This is AMC! It's rumored that perhaps these were functional on other Von Piranha AMXs. (Photo Courtesy Scott Lachenauer)

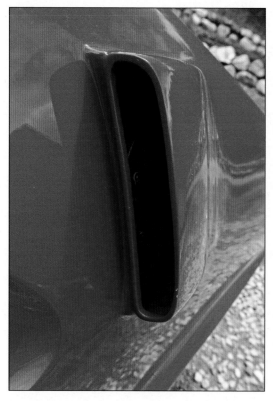

air-conditioning unit that dumped air onto your head, although both surviving cars seem to contradict that theory. Either way, they're unique in the muscle-car world as no other stock or Day 2 cars seemed to have had them.

Although not as egregious as putting scoops on the roof, these rear C-pillar scoops were reminiscent of those found on 1967 and 1968 Shelby Mustangs. (Photo Courtesy Scott Lachenauer)

These hood slits were likely created to let heat escape the engine compartment. But what about the rain and snow in Colorado? (Photo Courtesy Scott Lachenauer)

The stock AMX hood featured alterations in the form of the bulge sides being slit open in the shape of the letter "L." The Ls pointed inward and had hood pins stamped at the inward-most point. Exterior badging was minimal and didn't announce this species, but the promotional photos with Ron Hunter show either a vinyl or painted white Von Piranha callout on the front fenders.

Von Piranhas dipped their fins into the super-car world with what was present under the hood. The surviving cars are both Go Pak AMC 390s topped with a 950-cfm Holley 3-barrel carburetor sitting on a Group 19 R4B intake. Group 19 is the category American Motors Corporation consolidated its speed parts into and offered to the general public. The surviving red Von Piranha had a set of headers and slotted mags identical to the wheels seen on Ron Hunter's car. Scripted into the intake was the phrase "AMX PIRANHA." It's unclear if the gold/red car had the same treatment.

Ron Hunter

To date, only a handful of publicity photos exist of Ron Hunter's 1968 Von Piranha AMX. Ron's road-racing career began in 1957 when he ran an MG at La Junta Raceway in La Junta, Colorado. Ron was

Ron Hunter, a local and occasional Trans-Am racer, sits behind the wheel of a 1968 Von Piranha AMX at Continental Divide Raceway. (Photo Courtesy John A. Grissinger Family Archives)

active throughout the 1950s and 1960s and campaigned Alfas and Lotuses entering the Trans-Am series in 1966. In 1969, he ran 8 of the 12 Trans-Am races in a Javelin and brought home a best run of seventh at Riverside in October. The car wore sponsorship from the Denver AMC Dealers and had four names attributed on the rear quarter panel: Fred Von, Vic Hebert, Bob Bundy, and Fred Rike. It's unclear if Fred Von was the namesake for the Von Piranha.

It's believed that Hunter campaigned the AMX in the historic photos through Thoroughbred Motor Co. and may have been employed by them. The car purportedly ran at Continental Divide Raceway, although no shots of the car in action have been located.

Our Feature Car

The history of this car can be traced back through two owners. Wayne Sauer owned the car for 30-plus years after he purchased it from the previous owner, who purchased the car as a two-year-old used car. Mike Singer, a friend of Wayne's, always knew he had a peculiar AMX, but it wasn't until they were chatting one day that he heard the name "Piranha AMX." Simply based on curiosity and a desire to attempt to research the car, Wayne offered Mike a chance to purchase the long-dormant AMX.

When Mike rounded up the cash, he brought the Piranha home and sunk his teeth into the new unusual car. The AMX began life as a Go Pack performance machine, engorged with a 390-ci, 315-hp powerplant that was mated to a BorgWarner M12 3-speed automatic. It also had a Twin-Grip rear, the "handling suspension," and power front disc and rear drum brakes. The 30 years that Wayne owned it were extremely gentle on the AMX. It was rust-free and had a scant 24,000 rounds on the odometer.

For Mike, the hunt for information was gathered mostly by word of mouth from the prior owners, and Walt's memory served as the backbone of what's been gathered.

To Be Continued...

The period photographs of the Piranha AMX serve as the only historical reference to these cars. John A. Grissinger was there that day at Continental Divide Raceway and is responsible for these fantastic shots. Scouring online through historic newspapers or old dealership promotional ads has yielded not a drop in the bucket as to who definitively offered the Von Piranha AMX. The gold car (originally red) has disappeared from the spotlight, while Mike and Wayne's AMC has traded hands twice since the former parted with the car in 2015.

Time is running out on firsthand accounts of this incredibly rare species. Will more Piranhas spawn from this story and devour the muscle-car world in the coming years? We'll just have to bait the hook and wait.

Overall, the 1968 Von Piranha AMX still has more questions than answers. Perhaps this story will help put more facts into the history of this unique zone/dealer option. (Photo Courtesy John A. Grissinger Family Archives)

1969 PONTIAC GOLDEN SABRE AND 1970 MAGNUM 400s

By Wes Eisenschenk

Bill Knafel holds court while puffing on a pipe on the showroom floor of Bill Knafel Pontiac. Flanking Mr. Knafel are a pair of 1970 GTO Judges and a 1970 Tempest Magnum 400. (Photo Courtesy Knafel Family Archives)

Bill Knafel's path toward muscle-car notoriety was similar to many of his contemporaries in the 1950s. Fresh off a booming postwar economy, Bill purchased an established dealership named Anderson Pontiac located in Akron, Ohio, in 1959. Pontiac automobiles had been flourishing with the new Wide Track offerings, and it was a great time to get into sales. However, it was Bill's next foray into owning a dealership that got him national attention: drag racing.

Little is known about the 1959 Pontiac Catalina station wagon that Bill sponsored. However, all of that changed when "Akron" Arlen Vanke walked through the door in 1961 after he heard about the new 421 Super Duty engine that Bill had on a stand at Anderson Pontiac.

Arlen Vanke

Three years prior at the ninth-annual NASCAR International Safety and Performance Trials, Vanke paced his 1958 Chevrolet Impala over the flying-mile course to a speed of 125.786 mph on the Daytona Beach sand. In doing so, he received the Daytona Beach Chamber of Congress Century Club certificate for his accomplishment. Vanke campaigned a '55 Chevy on local and East Coast drag strips after his flying-mile days. However, it was on this day in Akron that changed his career path forever. Owner and salesman Bill Knafel sold Arlen on the benefits of purchasing a new 1962 421 Super Duty Pontiac as well as racing with Knafel Anderson sponsorship.

Bill Abraham, a 22-year-old local racer, had recently "retired" from drag racing and joined Vanke at Anderson Pontiac in the summer of 1962 and was part of the crew on Arlen's 421 Super Duty. Vanke's new red 1962 421 Super Duty Pontiac carried the Tin Indian moniker.

Knafel Pontiac Drag Racing

To say that Bill Knafel left an undeniable mark in drag racing is an understatement. With Vanke and Abraham campaigning Bill's Pontiacs, the record books were rewritten. Vanke noted that the 1962 Catalina convertible that he campaigned for Knafel (one of five 1962s that Vanke campaigned) never lost in the C/Stock Automatic category.

The murderers row of high-powered Ponchos that Vanke campaigned read like the heart of the 1927 Yankees lineup: a 1962 421 Super Duty Catalina, 1963 Papoose One Super Duty Tempest Wagon (1 of 6), and 1963 421 Super Duty Catalina "Swiss Cheese" (1 of 12).

Arlen left for greener pastures after GM pulled out of sanctioned drag racing, and Bill brought in the biggest name and die-hard Pontiac holdout: Arnie "The Farmer" Beswick. Beswick had a fleet of potent Pontiacs, which had "Bill Knafel's Anderson Pontiac" on its sheet metal, continuing the assault on the competition.

In total, 42 drag cars wore sponsorship from Knafel Pontiac from 1959 through 1971.

An iconic fleet of Bill Knafel Anderson Pontiac drag cars campaigned by Arnie "the Farmer" Beswick are loaded up and ready to hit the next drag strip. No one represented Pontiac longer or better than the Farmer. (Photo Courtesy Arnie Beswick)

"Akron" Arlen Vanke (left), Bill Knafel (middle), and "Abie" Bill Abraham became an unbeatable trio at the drag strip and in the showroom. (Photo Courtesy Knafel Family Archives)

Super Cars

While Knafel Pontiacs tore up the drag strip, a new genre of the muscle car began to take shape in the mid-1960s: the super car.

Since the beginning of the automobile, engines expired and were replaced by either the same kind of motor or something with a little more oomph.

During the 1960s, the manufacturers began doing this with specially equipped factory race cars. These cars were built based on mandates by sanctioning drag-racing bodies to compete in "stock" classes. Not all these cars made it onto the drag strip, as knowing a guy at a high-performance dealership could land you a potent street weapon.

Detroit dealership Royal Pontiac is often credited as the creator of the super car. Royal would "Bobcat" Grand Prixs, Tempests, Catalinas, GTOs, and later Firebirds to create street rockets for customers. "Bobcatting" entailed anything from adding speed parts to a full engine swap.

The first two Chevrolet dealerships to roll out programs of engine-swapping for customers were Dana Chevrolet and Nickey Chevrolet. The earliest of these conversions that utilized the Camaro platform date back to October 1966.

1969 Pontiac GTO Golden Sabre

If ever there was a car with an enigma, it is the 1969 Golden Sabre.

Knafel's first cannonade into Super Car production is as mysterious as Amelia Earhart's disappearance. A lone photo exists of the Golden Sabre in what appears to be Polar White with gold striping.

The white hue was painted over with a Pearlescent White at the dealership. The striping, reminiscent of the 1969 GTO Judge, ran in a U-shape design along the side of the car. The upper stripe tailed up around the rear side glass, while the lower portion ran slightly above the bottom of the fender/rocker/rear quarters. A single gold stripe traversed the full hood and roof, and possibly the decklid too. The front fender announced "Golden Sabre" with a sword underneath the hand-painted text. Directly underneath the sword were the words "SUPER TUNED." The car ran on Hurst polished wheels.

Under the hood was Pontiac's mythical Ram Air V that had dyno ratings at Pontiac in the 500-hp range. The crated Ram Air Vs arrived at Knafel minus carburation. Both automatics and manuals were

This lone photo exists of a 1969 GTO Golden Sabre on the lot at Knafel Pontiac. Very little is known about these cars, and not a single car has been documented as still existing. (Photo Courtesy Knafel Family Archives)

alleged to have been produced, while either the 3.90 or the stump-pulling 4.33s could be had out back.

Bob Knafel professed years later that a scant 12 were produced. To date, not a single Golden Sabre has been located and verified.

1970 Tempest Magnum 400

Following his freshman campaign into super-car converting, Knafel offered the Tempest Magnum 400.

Perhaps taking a lesson from the Golden Sabre, Bob Knafel created a launch party for the Magnum 400s. Knafel introduced his new offering to the masses on two consecutive nights, December 19 and 20, 1969, with Knafel racer Norm Tanner in attendance.

The Magnum 400s consisted of the lighter Tempest body (3,200 pounds) that sported a 400-ci, 350-hp Pontiac engine that was mated to a 4-speed transmission with a 3.90 gearset. Knafel stated in advertisements that the cars came equipped with a Hurst shifter, GTO suspension, Mag II wheels, dual exhaust, and custom carpeting. The ads for the Magnum 400 ran from December 1969 through May 1970.

Aesthetically, the Magnum 400 wasn't much different from a

Bill Knafel Pontiac formally announced the Magnum 400 in the Akron, Ohio, newspapers. For less than $3,000, a Tempest could receive a 400 with 350-hp, a 4-speed transmission, and 3.91 gears. This is more bang for the buck than the previous year's Motor Trend car of the year, the 1969 Plymouth Road Runner. (Photo Courtesy Knafel Family Archives)

production Tempest, although it did have the carryover 1969 Judge stripe and a pair of Magnum 400 decal callouts on the front fenders and on the passenger's side of the decklid.

Options were available à la carte on the 400, including a Rally steering wheel, Keystone mag wheels, a hood-mounted tachometer, chrome tailpipe collectors, white-sidewall tires, Rally cluster gauges, a push-button radio, an AM/FM stereo radio, Hooker headers, racing spark plugs, an Accel Performance ignition, and chrome hood tie-downs.

A salesman (or potential customer) paces a Magnum 400 through winter conditions in Ohio. Such was life for a midyear unveiling. The Tempest borrowed the 1969 GTO Judge stripe kit for its 1970 model. (Photo Courtesy Knafel Family Archives)

A salesman takes calls in the offices at Knafel Pontiac. This close-up fender photo is the clearest image of the Magnum 400 decal. No surviving cars have been documented at this time. (Photo Courtesy Knafel Family Archives)

In later years, Bob Knafel noted that 50 Magnum 400s were created. Not a single car has been verified as being part of this program.

Lasting Legacy

If a grand total of 62 custom cars were created by Knafel Pontiac, it's almost a guarantee that one has survived. Old classified ads from Akron, Ohio, seem to indicate that a host of these cars were offered for resale throughout the 1970s. In all likelihood, some of the cars lost their identity through customization or repainting. Being a Midwest promotion, it's logical to assume many were lost due to the harsh weather conditions and salted roads.

If a true Golden Sabre or Magnum 400 is found, it will be a celebrated day in the land of Pontiac enthusiasts. Knafel Pontiac remains a celebrated dealership long after its doors closed in 1975. A host of the drag cars campaigned by Knafel racers exist in collections and can been seen at Pontiac reunions and muscle-car shows. Bob Knafel set out to make his mark when he purchased Anderson Pontiac, and there's no doubt that he met and exceeded that goal.

1969 427 DALE CHEVROLET NOVA *RAMPAGE*

By Wes Eisenschenk

Some names represent a car well and others don't. The transparent dome over the dual carburetors leads me to believe that "Rampage" fits this car perfectly. (Photo Courtesy David Everhardy)

One wouldn't think that a location with a seasonal climate, such as Wisconsin, would be a good fit for a Nova super car. With a racing season between mid-April and late October, there isn't much time to stretch the legs of a performance machine. Somehow, David Eberhardy found a way to rack up 117,000 miles in four years on his 427-powered Nova.

A few years earlier, David was at a car show at State Fair Park in West Allis, Wisconsin. Some of the local dealerships were on hand to promote upcoming iron that would be on display in showroom floors and out on the lots. While canvassing the area, David saw a beastly little machine that high-volume muscle-car seller Dale Chevrolet had on hand. Dale Chevrolet's display featured an L78 1968 Nova that was converted into a 427-powered monster.

The super-car rage had taken over the biggest and best high-performance dealerships in years prior, as places such as Grand Spaulding Dodge shoehorned 440-ci of displacement between Dodge Dart fenders. Bob Tasca in Rhode Island found a way to fit a 428 police interceptor engine into 1967 Mustangs.

With GM's engine-displacement ban on compact and midsize

cars, Oldsmobile moved some Cutlasses over to Hurst for 455 conversions. Chevy stalwarts Don Yenko, Dick Harrell, Dana Chevrolet, and Nickey Chevrolet began to yank 350- and 396-ci engines out of Camaros, Chevelles, and Novas, and swap in 427s that were meant for the Corvette and the full-size lineup. As much as everyone today thinks that super cars were built and delivered everywhere, it was really the Midwest and the Rust Belt that carried most of the water during the height of the dealer-swapped performance era. The 1968 Nova 427 wasn't meant to be for David at the time, but he earmarked the moment and mentally noted how much of an impression the car made on him.

While things heated up in the world of the super car, the factories were getting in-tune with what the market was shifting toward: wild and extravagant-looking muscle cars. David absolutely loved the new look of the 1969 Z/28 Camaro and had to have one, so he headed over to the dealership and put in an order for a Fathom Green car with white stripes. Unfortunately for him, production was backed up at GM, and it took 10 months for the Camaro to arrive.

Possibly perturbed with how long it took for the car to arrive, or because he still thought about that Nova, after 10 months of Camaro ownership, he headed over to Dale Chevrolet to see what they could do to help him scratch that itch.

Dale Chevrolet had grown into one of the largest-volume Corvette dealerships in the country. In 1969 alone, it sold 300 new and 200 used Corvettes. Along with up to 50 SS 396 Chevelles on the lot at one time, Dale Chevrolet was bursting at the seams in the high-performance marketplace.

As he had hoped, Dale Chevrolet was still converting Novas to 427 power. Around June 1969, the dealership began promotional work on the super-car conversions under the term "Dale Dusters," either not knowing or caring that Plymouth came out with the Duster nameplate that fall. Dale advertised, "Specializing in 427 Camaros, Novas, and Chevelles — Dale Sets the Pace in New and Used Cars."

Under a July 25, 1969, advertisement for 1969 Camaros, it added, "Dale Dusters, 427s, Z/28s, and SS 396s." It's unclear how much of a shot that Dale Chevrolet injected into the super-car genre, but it was there to play the game.

At the dealership, Dave was told that to create his dream Nova, he had to pay the $3,600 that was required to purchase an L78 1970 Nova SS. He felt that it was as good of a time as any to trade in the

Dale Chevrolet was no stranger to high-performance auto sales. It sold Yenkos through its dealer network as well.

Camaro because the clutch was going out, so he made the commitment to own a Nova super car.

Dale Chevrolet prided itself on having an abundance of inventory, so Dave had his pick of the litter when it came to building his factory hot rod. Not looking to go broke but still have a good-looking car, Dave selected an Astro Blue, blue bench-seat, 4-speed Nova for his super-car template. For Dale Chevrolet to upgrade him to its biggest Rat motor available, he had to pay an additional $600. Out the door, close to $4,200 was spent on his boulevard bruiser.

With his dream Nova now secured, it was time to add some custom touches. A set of headers was added as well as a tunnel ram and one of the coolest transparent scoops that was available. Like every cool cat in the day, Dave gave his car a name: *Rampage*. Clearly, with a machine of this caliber, you wouldn't consider driving it all year long, right?

Wrong! Over the next four years, David racked up 117,000 miles—rain or shine, snow or sleet. One would think that it has to be some sort of super-car mileage record. As the gas crunch of 1973 began to rear its ugly head, and with the paltry 11 mpg David got with the Nova, he made the tough decision to move on from his beloved super car.

In waiting was one of David's buddies, Randy Moze, who bought the car for the steal-of-the-century price of $300! You read that correctly.

Randy only had it for a couple of years when he too couldn't afford to keep gas in the thing and had to sell it.

David Everhardy's beautiful Nova sits on the beaches of Southern California. When David said he put 117,000 miles on the Nova, he was telling the truth. (Photo Courtesy David Everhardy)

1970 DICK HARRELL CAMARO

By Rick Nelson

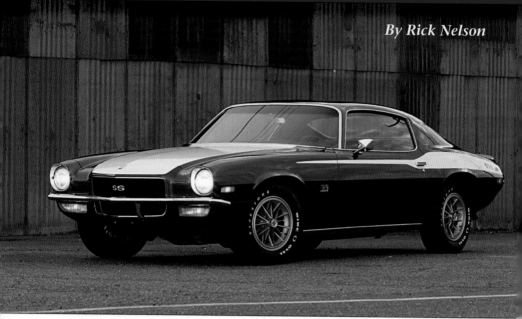

A set of Kelsey-Hayes Stripper 15x7s rotate with original Firestone Wide Oval rubber on them. Dick capped off the conversion by whitening out the hood and using the patent side stripe he used on his 1969 Camaros. (Photo Courtesy Eric English)

Any high-performance Chevrolet enthusiast will recognize the name Dick Harrell, or "Mr. Chevrolet," as he was known later in life. Born on October 4, 1932, in Phoenix, Arizona, as Richard M. Harrell, Dick had mechanics and engineering in his blood. By the age of 14, after he moved to Carlsbad, New Mexico, he began racing sprint cars. At 17, he graduated to stock cars. However, at age 18, he found himself employed by the U.S. Army and was trained to work on aircraft engines and airframes for light single-engine aircraft that were used in Korea and Oklahoma.

After his stint in the military, Harrell moved back to Carlsbad and became a fierce competitor, drag racing a '56 Chevrolet throughout south Texas. In 1961, Harrell was unstoppable in his Chevrolet and won most every event in which he participated. He began to receive appearance money from various tracks that wanted him there and to help draw racing fans. By 1962, he moved up the ranks and became a professional racer while campaigning a 1962 Chevy, and later a 1963 427 Z-11 Impala. At the 1963 AHRA Winter Nationals, Dick waded through the stiff competition to garnish the Super Stock Eliminator win, which propelled him into national fame. He went on to set many NHRA and AHRA records in the following years.

In 1964, Ford dominated the track with the 427-powered Fairlane Thunderbolt. Chevrolet had nothing available to use to compete against that car, and for a time, it lacked wins. That was until Harrell installed the 427 mystery motor that was borrowed from the NASCAR guys into the newly released Chevrolet Chevelle. Using all the mechanical and engineering tricks that he learned over the years, he made it fit, and he made it run.

Chevrolet pulled out all of its backing from racing in February 1963, which killed the opportunity to compete for many team cars and others who used its backing. Most of these teams and drivers went to Ford and Chrysler because they still supported racing. With Chrysler coming on hard with its newly introduced 426 Hemi, this made it very tough for the Chevrolet teams. However, someone forgot to tell Mr. Chevrolet, as he continued to run and win with the bowties throughout the rest of his career.

Nickey Chevrolet

In later years, starting around 1966, Harrell wasn't satisfied with winning at national tracks and wanted to win on the street as well. He teamed up with Nickey Chevrolet, which was in Chicago, Illinois. Nickey used Harrell's engineering and building techniques to create some of the meanest street cars of the day.

In 1967, Chevrolet introduced the Camaro. Using the previous year's introduction of the 427-ci street engine, it was only natural for Harrell to install it in the new car. It is widely believed that Harrell was the first person to ever install a 427 in a Camaro for a dealer, which then sold it to the public.

Yenko Chevrolet

Harrell once again made another move, this time to East St. Louis, Illinois, where he opened the Dick Harrell Performance Center. It later moved to Kansas City, Missouri. Due to the affiliation with Nickey Chevrolet, Harrell was introduced to Don Yenko, who persuaded

Harrell to convert cars through his Canonsburg, Pennsylvania, dealership as well. Dick was the catalyst for Don Yenko entering into the world of drag racing.

Fred Gibb Chevrolet

During this time, he also met Fred Gibb, who owned Fred Gibb Chevrolet. Gibb, who already had a racing team, jumped at the chance to work with Harrell. Through the association with these three big players, Harrell built and modified many 350, 427, and 454 Novas, Camaros, Chevelles, Vegas, and at least one Monte Carlo and one El Camino. Harrell converted many well-known 427 automatic Novas in 1968 and was instrumental in putting the 1968 COPO Nova program and 1969 Camaro ZL1 package together for Fred Gibb. Harrell continued to be successful on the street and the track until his untimely death in 1971 due to a tragic racing accident.

Inside, it was business as usual in the Camaro. The automatic on the console rowed a 400 Turbo transmission. (Photo Courtesy Eric English)

1970 Dick Harrell LS6 454 Camaro

Of all of the Dick Harrell cars that were built, only a few 1970 race Camaros are known to have been campaigned, and only one is known to have been built for street use. However, as widely known as Dick Harrell was, it is likely that there was more than one built, although this particular car is the only one that has ever been rumored to have existed or been found.

The whereabouts of this car remained unknown until late 2002. It all started when I, a member of Yenko.net, saw a clipping of a 1973 classified ad for a 1970 Dick Harrell LS6 454-converted Camaro. Until then, I had never heard of a 1970 Dick Harrell Camaro—only the earlier Camaros. What made it even more interesting was that the car had been for sale in New Ulm, Minnesota, which is 45 minutes from my home. Since I was somewhat bored and curious, I set out to try and find whatever happened to the car. Numerous phone calls, visits, and emails netted me nothing more than rumors.

Hunting the Harrell Camaro

I met with Ron Bentz, who was a sheriff's deputy in Brown County, Minnesota, which is where New Ulm is located. Ron had posted some restoration questions on Yenko.net, and after receiving little help, I decided to contact him privately and answer some of his restoration queries. This led to a friendship and a trust to the point where I confided in Bentz about the Camaro.

He distinctly remembered a green Camaro with white stripes that tore up the streets in the early 1970s but had simply disappeared. Bentz was unsure if it was a Harrell car, but he said it could have been a Motion Camaro as well. He could not remember how the striping was done for sure—only that they were white. At the time the ad was placed in 1973, the car had only 5,400 miles on it.

Bentz used his talents as a police officer to investigate. Astonishingly, only two days later, Bentz contacted me and said that he located the owner of the car. He provided the owner's name, address, and phone number. He was the same person who had owned it since the early 1970s. He had drag and street raced the car heavily, but upon his return from Vietnam, he had lost interest in the car. It sat in his secondary garage on his property where he drove it once a month to keep it clean and running. The car didn't have street use after 1973 until it was found in 2002.

I contacted the individual, who happened to be the fourth owner. We discussed the car at length on that first call, but I was very careful not to show too much excitement. It took me over nine months of phone calls to gain his confidence.

Hiding in Plain Sight

Over time, I made several excuses that I was going to be in or near New Ulm and would like to see the car, but the owner kept me hanging just enough that I was unable to make it work out. That is, until one day when I received a phone call from him. He told me he was going to take the car out, wash it, and run it, and I was invited to come look at it. Upon my arrival, there was the car, sitting in the front yard on a main highway where no one had ever stopped to inquire about it. It was like it had been kept in a time capsule and showed no signs of wear.

Chevrolet's vaunted LS6 454-ci 450-hp big-block resides between the fenders of the Harrell Camaro. This engine was only found in the Chevelle for the 1970 production year. Harrell valve-cover decals ensure the quality and durability of the engine maker. (Photo Courtesy Eric English)

Authenticity

After much discussion, I made it clear to the owner that I wanted to buy the car from him and be the next caretaker, but first I wanted to authenticate it through my friend Dennis Hartweg, one of the leading experts on Fred Gibb and Dick Harrell cars and history. Hartweg's father worked for Gibb Chevrolet, and Dennis had a vast knowledge of these cars.

Dennis was quite sure that the car had no affiliation to Fred Gibb but that it was a special-order Camaro sold through the high-performance dealer Van Chevrolet in Shawnee Mission, Kansas.

It began life as an SS 350 Camaro and was modified by the Harrell Performance Center after the owner took delivery. We struck a deal on the price, but the night before I was to take over ownership of the car, the seller raised the price. I could no longer afford the car, so the Camaro was purchased by my good friend Chad Blomberg. Sadly, Dennis Hartweg passed away from a heart attack shortly after the car's purchase and was never able to see the car, although his widow was instrumental in helping us further authenticate the car.

Minnesota History on the Harrell Camaro

Through much research, Chad and I traced the car back to the second owner who lived in Marshall, Minnesota. It was that owner who installed the chrome Sizzler Superior mag wheels. Harrell was a Superior dealer, so up until that point, it was assumed that Harrell had installed the wheels.

During the conversation about the wheels, I asked the second owner what wheels were originally on the car.

"Some sort of funky cast-aluminum wire wheel," he replied. "They weren't Keystones but started with a K."

"Kelsey-Hayes?" I asked.

"Yes, that was it," he said.

Then, he said, "Hang on a moment" and left his office.

He remembered he had stacked them in a corner of his warehouse, and much to our astonishment, Chad and I were able to see the original wheels and tires from the car for the first time since the early 1970s. Although the owner held them for ransom, Chad purchased them and reunited them with the car.

Keeping it as Original as Possible

Chad and I spent many hours cleaning the years of dust and a few years of road grime from the car without ever actually restoring any part of the car. During this time, we contacted Dave Libby who had worked in Harrell's shop until 1970. He did not convert this car, as he had already left the Dick Harrell Performance Center, but he did remember it. He stated that the way we found the car with the white side stripe, stripper wheels, "454" painted numerals on the quarter panels, white hood stripe, spoiler, red heater hoses, and the strange steel tubing wrapped around the header pipe for the choke was exactly how Harrell's shop had built it. He said that a person nicknamed "Oops" was responsible for painting the 454 numerals on the side of the car. The Camaro also retained its original Dick Harrell medallions.

To this day, this 1970 LS6 converted Camaro remains the only known Harrell-converted 1970 Camaro in existence and maintains its appearance as a time capsule in a very well-known car collection in the Northwest.

The original owner's name and whereabouts have never been found, and he only owned the car for a few months before he sold it.

Dick Harrell personified Chevrolet performance, and this Camaro is one of the many unique and rare Harrell conversions.

1970 DICK HARRELL CHEVROLET VEGA

By Wes Eisenschenk

American Hot Rod Association (AHRA) Driver of the Decade Dick Harrell created this insurance buster for 1970. Almost immediately, the Chevrolet Vega became the vehicle of choice for drag racers due to its compact size. (Photo Courtesy the Enthusiast Network)

If one was tasked with creating a Mount Rushmore of the muscle-car era, there are several names that would end up on the cutting-room floor. Attempting to whittle down a list that includes company presidents; drag, road-course, and oval-track racers; dealership principles; zone managers; marketing gurus; magazine columnists; and super tuners, someone would be bound to be left out. However, if I were encumbered with such a task, and after laboring with intensive thought, I'd offer the following: Carroll Shelby, John DeLorean, Bunkie Knudsen, and Dick Harrell.

Mr. Chevrolet

For most, Dick Harrell was a famous drag racer who campaigned Chevrolets throughout the 1960s. For those with an ear to the ground, Dick Harrell was the straw that stirred the Chevrolet super-car drink.

Dick "Mr. Chevrolet" Harrell was born in Phoenix, Arizona, and grew up in New Mexico. That's not necessarily a place you'd think a person who became synonymous with lightning-fast Chevrolets might be from, but Dick cut his teeth running Micro Midgets in Arizona and New Mexico in the mid-1950s. After a few years in the army, a stint in Korea, and being stationed at a helicopter base in Lawton, Oklahoma, Harrell picked up the sport of drag racing and returned to Carlsbad, New Mexico, after his service to the government was completed. It was back home in Carlsbad where Dick took a budding hobby and made it a career by successfully drag racing Chevrolets.

Super-Tuner

Harrell's success in campaigning Chevrolets during and after the brand pulled out of sanctioned racing gave him name recognition nationwide. One dealership that recognized his talents was Nickey Chevrolet, in Chicago, Illinois. At Nickey, Dick was the performance advisor, and he raced a 1966 Nova. He was at Nickey when the Camaro debuted and was likely the first person to drop a 427-ci engine in Chevrolet's new pony car. After Nickey was the job of super car–converting Don Yenko's first batch of 1967 Camaros in East St. Louis, Illinois.

Harrell bet on himself in early 1968 and opened Dick Harrell Performance Center at 11114 Hickman Mills Dr. in Kansas City, Missouri. In February 1970, he opened a second location at 403 E. Lohman Ave. in Santa Cruz, New Mexico. It was at the Kansas City location where he started carving out a name for himself.

In the July 1968 issue of *Super Stock and Drag Illustrated*, Harrell's shop was featured in an article called "Chevy Capital of the Midwest." The article stated that SS-packaged 396-ci, 375-hp (L78) Camaros and Chevelles were delivered to his location for 427 short-block transplants. Harrell offered an à la carte menu of performance goodies, including a Tri-Power intake ($285), an L-88 engine with aluminum heads ($626), a host of power adders, and stabilizing equipment to keep the car safe and hooked up. After a tour of the shop, a Camaro and Chevelle were packed up and shipped to Kansas City International Raceway where they were rung out to the tune of mid-12-second passes. The Chevelle had 43 miles on the odometer. That's not bad for a motor that wasn't broken in yet.

COPO Novas

Dick's next big splash came via the central office production order (COPO) and an association with longtime Chevrolet dealer Fred Gibb. Under Vince Piggens, GM's president at the time, Gibb ordered 50 new 1968 Novas that featured the 3-speed Turbo Hydra-Matic 400 automatic transmission. With the 50 cars on order, the NHRA approved the modified Novas for stock/automatic classes in the series. A handful of these brutes made their way to Dick Harrell Performance Center for 427 swaps to weaponize the Chevy II into arguably the fiercest street car ever.

1969

Harrell, using the COPO system, continued to produce 427-powered super cars directly through his General Motors pipeline (COPO order 9561) and continued to swap 396-ci, 375-hp cars through Dick Harrell Performance Center. Mr. Chevrolet also continued to super-tune anything that came through the door, with records that show 'Cudas and GTOs getting the Harrell touch. As the calendar year rolled over, Harrell had another trick up his sleeve in what was his parting offering to the muscle-car era.

Harrell Vega

The calendar year of 1970 is pointed to as being the high-water mark but also the beginning of the end of the muscle-car era. GM had lifted its displacement ban and allowed for 454-equipped Chevrolet Chevelles, Monte Carlos, and El Caminos; and 455-displaced Pontiac GTOs, Buick Gran Sports, and Oldsmobile Cutlass machines to prowl the streets. As the manufacturers spoke out of one side of their mouth with big-cubed muscle cars, they also began to utter a different tone out of the other side with more compacts. It was in 1970 when cars like the AMC Gremlin, the Ford Maverick, and the Chevrolet Vega were created.

Car Craft magazine headed to Dick's shop in the fall of 1970 after rumors about a small-block sniper that Harrell had up his sleeve. As the worm began to turn on the muscle-car era, Dick was asked by a customer to convert a 1971 Chevrolet Vega into a 400-ci small-block street sweeper. The Vega was outfitted with TRW's new

When you need to slap something together quickly for Car Craft *magazine, this is what you come up with. (Photo Courtesy the Enthusiast Network)*

high-compression pistons (available in 11:1 or 12.5:1), a stock LT-1 solid-lifter camshaft, Poweready ignition, an Offenhauser manifold with a 1,000-cfm Carter Thermo-Quad, a Turbo Hydra-Matic transmission, and a 12-bolt narrowed 3.55 ring gear out of a Chevelle.

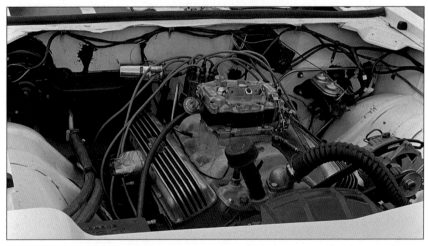

Dick Harrell wedged GM's all-new 400 small-block between the fenders to create a mini–Mighty Mouse of a monster. Who needs power brakes? (Photo Courtesy the Enthusiast Network)

The Vega ended up where most performance-oriented Vegas end up: at the drag strip. The car is seen here at Thompson Drag Raceway. (Photo Courtesy Charles Gilchrist)

To accommodate the 400, Harrell removed the K-member and repositioned the steering bracket 2.5 inches lower. The steering arm on the left side was lengthened the same amount by cutting the arm and adding another piece of metal. Harrell created his own cross-member for the vacant K-member.

A former owner retained the set of valve covers from the 1970 Dick Harrell Vega. No, they're not for sale!

Aesthetically, the car was Antique White and featured the familiar Dick Harrell side stripe in black, which was also utilized on the 1969 Camaros and 1970 Novas. The car sat atop a set of 6x15-inch Kelsey-Hayes 6-inch wheels with Firestone Wide Oval rubber. A black stinger stripe ran down the middle of the hood. The tail panel was blacked out to complete the look.

Performance

Car Craft staff brought the Vega to Kansas City International Raceway, where it cut a best time of 12.48 at 110.13 mph. The 6-inch wheels and 3.55 gearset contributed to the car not dipping into the 11s on street tires.

Marketing and First Owners

The Vega served for a spell as a marketing tool for Harrell, and one stop was at Harry May Chevrolet in Michigan. Harrell used his newly converted cars for grand openings at dealerships that carried Harrell parts and sold his cars.

The first official set of owners were Eddie Anderson and Jim Svetek. Jim campaigned the car and ran a best time of 11.25 at 128 mph at Thompson Dragway in Ohio. They campaigned the car together for four to five years before they sold it to a law-enforcement officer who bought the car for his son.

The car was rumored to have been repainted. There are also rumors of other Harrell-converted Vegas with evidence of one appearing with the white car at the Harry May Chevrolet grand opening. However, to this day, the *Car Craft*–tested 400-ci small-block Dick Harrell Vega has not been seen since.

1970½ CAMARO: HURST SUNSHINE SPECIAL

By Wes Eisenschenk

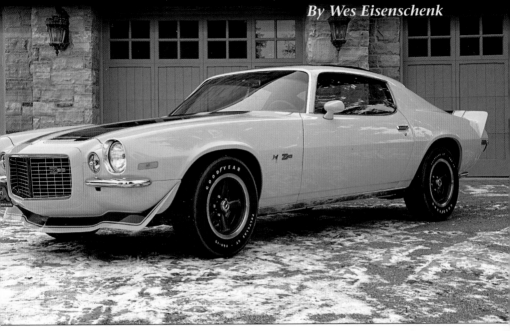

Although Hurst and Chevrolet collaborations were few and far between, the 1970½ Hurst Sunshine Special Camaro looked and acted the part. (Photo Courtesy Richard Truesdell)

When one thinks of Hurst Performance and George Hurst, the manufacturer Chevrolet doesn't often come to mind. Most of us think about the Hurst Oldsmobiles that were created intermittently between 1968 and 1984, while others recall the quarter-mile wheel-standing Hemi Barracudas that campaigned under the moniker *Hemi Under Glass*.

There were the occasional partnerships with Pontiac (the SSJ Grand Prix), Chrysler (the 300-H), Jeep (the Hurst Jeepster), Dodge/Plymouth (the BO23 and B029 Race Hemis), and AMC (the SC/Rambler), but there was nary a union between GM's most proficient automobile manufacturer and Detroit's most successful third-party super-car builder.

However, in 1970, Hurst built a pair of one-offs that were used for promotional and experimental purposes. These cars became the rarest Hurst-built cars of all.

Hurst Nova

In my previous book, I told the saga of the 1970 Hurst Nova. This was a giveaway car in the name-a-shifter contest that sought an official title for the new automatic gearbox offered by Hurst. Entry boxes were setup at parts stores, and thousands of name suggestions were entered. Hurst settled on "Hurst-A-Matic" and culled over 20 entrants who suggested a title. From there, one entrant was selected: a two-year-old boy from Cleveland, Ohio! Young Todd Trapnell and his family attended the 1970 NHRA U.S. Nationals, and they were handed the keys to the Nova at a banquet that weekend. Todd's father had entered multiple suggestions on behalf of his children. So, fortunately for Todd, his parents accepted the car on his behalf.

The Hurst Nova served as transportation for the Trapnells, but ultimately it wasn't large enough to transport the family and was sold in the early 1970s. It found its way to Thompson Dragway in the mid-1970s and into the hands of another party who had intentions of restoring it toward the end of the decade. It didn't come to fruition, and the car ended up in a junkyard that was later cleaned out. It was a sad end to the Hurst Nova, but it gave birth to another collaboration between Hurst and Chevrolet.

Dick Jesse

Michigan drag racer Dick Jesse thought the new Camaro was a great platform to build a quarter-mile car. Dick worked at Royal Pontiac

Dick Jesse may have been out of drag racing, but he still had name recognition. I hope the display board for Merollis Chevy City didn't scratch the paint. (Photo Courtesy Merollis Chevrolet)

Dick Jesse peers over the roof of the Unswitchable *GTO as he makes a pass at Motor City Drag-way. (Photo Courtesy NHRA)*

and had been at the genesis of the altered-wheelbase era and campaigned a 1965 GTO named *Mr. Unswitchable*. Dick suffered a nasty crash and rolled his 1965 GTO six times at 134 mph during a test at Motor City Dragway in October 1966. Jesse's *Funny Card* campaigned across the Midwest in match races via the sanctioning bodies of the AHRA and NASCAR's drag-racing series. By the late 1960s, Jesse stopped running the Funnies and sold bowtie iron at Merollis Chevrolet.

Perhaps leveling down from a Funny Car to a doorslammer would keep him out of the hospital.

1970½ Camaro

After the 18-month auto-workers strike ended, the Camaro finally made its debut midseason with its share of applause and jeers. The 1970½ Camaro was the last time a big-block (396/402) sat between the fenders of the pony car, as more performance-oriented small-blocks guided the Chevy to the end of the muscle-car era.

One of those nasty little small-blocks that was available in the Camaro was the all-new LT-1.

Performance-wise, the LT-1 was only outpowered by the 396/402-ci engine, which made its last hurrah in the Camaro. With 350 ci, the LT-1 featured four-bolt mains, a forged-steel crank, forged 11.0.1 pistons, an aluminum intake, and a healthy Holley carburetor when

The hot news for 1970½ was the introduction of the potent LT-1 into the Chevrolet lineup. Only the Corvette, Z/28, and COPO Nova could be had with the snappy motor. (Photo Courtesy Richard Truesdell)

optioned with the Z/28 package. A total of 8,733 Camaros, 1,287 Corvettes, and 177 Novas (COPO 9010) received this engine. Horsepower was rated at 360 in the Camaro and Nova and 370 in the Corvette.

With the hot, new engine package, Dick ordered his car in May 1970 through Merollis Chevrolet, where he was a salesman on 8-Mile Road and Gratiot Avenue in East Detroit. The LT-1 was paired with the 3-speed automatic transmission and a deep set of 4.10s with Positraction and drag racing in mind.

However, before Dick could lay the wood to the Daytona Yellow Camaro, neighboring Hurst Performance came calling.

Sunshine and Lollipops

The new Camaro was ideal for Hurst to conduct a few styling exercises. With Dick's blessing, the Camaro made its way to the Hurst Performance Research, Inc., location in Royal Oak, Michigan, for some minor procedures. With Hurst being known for shifters, that was the first item to be upgraded on the automatic transmission.

Shift This

Hurst looked to replicate the Dual Gate unit that was offered at the beginning of 1963 and picked up by the Oldsmobile and Pontiac manufacturers for production model use as an option. With tooling from four separate manual Hurst units, a single shifter was created that allowed the transmission to be left in drive or via the gate to keep the car in a single gear for manual shifting at higher RPM. This allowed for regular driving or for a more robust, performance-oriented experience.

Sunshine

Another modification made to the Camaro that separated it completely from production units was the addition of a sunroof. Across all manufacturers, the advent of the sunroof, which was popularized on the Volkswagen Beetle, began to appear on muscle-car models.

In 1967, the Mercury Cougar XR-G had cars converted by American Sunroof Company (ASC), and Dodge added the option to its Chargers in 1969 through the same company. Dodge sent a total of 391 Chargers to ASC's Detroit facility in 1969 for conversion.

There were no factory-produced sunroof 1970½ Camaros aside from this one-off. (Photo Courtesy Richard Truesdell)

Sensing a trend in the industry and being capable of converting large numbers of automobiles, Hurst smelled an opportunity with the 1970 Camaro. Dick's Z/28 received a sunroof along with a flip-up deflector to help reduce buffeting when the car was at speed. The final touches included "H" badging on the fenders and glove box as the official transformation to the Sunshine Special became complete.

After completion, the Camaro was sent to Chevrolet's engineering department for aerodynamic testing. The car had experimental front and rear spoilers grafted onto the body and went through a series of aero tests to see how added downforce affected the Z/28. It's alleged that this was for Trans-Am racing, but it doesn't make sense to install a sunroof and deflector, which would add weight. In all likelihood, Hurst looked for a bid on mass conversions for Chevrolet to consider.

Satisfied or unsatisfied with the results, the Camaro was returned to Dick. He promptly got the Z/28 onto the strip, which was his intention in the first place.

Legacy

Dick sold the car after a year of use. Over the years, the Sunshine Special was sold and resold with its heritage intact. A restoration of the Camaro was completed in 1988, and it now resides in the Rick Hendrick Collection.

It's been rumored for years that there were two Hurst Sunshine Special siblings. However, records of these cars haven't been published, or possibly, the cars were used for other experimental work by Hurst. Until they're located, this car will stand alone as the sole Hurst Sunshine Special Camaro.

1970 PONTIAC LEMANS JURY CARTER AND STAMPEDE

By Duncan Brown

It's always great to see our friends north of the border create awesome iron. The Carter and Stampede LeMans Jury was a special-batch-order vehicle that was painted in Palladium Silver. (Photo Courtesy Duncan Brown)

An ideal combination of image, price, and performance spurred sales of the inexpensive 1968 Plymouth Road Runner. Plymouth siphoned sales from the more expensive Pontiac GTO. Pontiac responded with a stripped, budget-friendly Tempest package named the "E/T," which was an abbreviation for "elapsed time."

The E/T equaled Road Runner pricing with a 350 H.O. engine that cost less than the base GTO 400. Pontiac Motor Division Manager John DeLorean angrily vetoed the 350 and proclaimed, "This is a 400-ci world!"

DeLorean reworked the E/T into the premium Judge option for the 1969 GTO. The Judge didn't just revert to the 400—it jumped to the Ram Air III 400. Bye-bye, budget! The spoiler-clad, striped, eye-searing Judge was announced in December 1968.

Tempest H.O. 350

Pontiac offered inexpensive small-displacement performance, but Pontiac's Tempest 350 H.O. lacked the identity of the Road Runner or GTO. The vinyl side stripe was frequently deleted by buyers.

What if kids could get a bargain car with Judge looks? The dealer-special Jury answered this question prior to a mid-1970-model-year trend. Factory small-block junior muscle soon gained wild attention and grabbed the appearance that was usually reserved for big-blocks. The Jury addressed this market at the start of the 1970 model year.

1970 Big-Block Packaging

The year 1970 was a high-water mark for wild-looking beasts that ran high-compression big-block engines. Bright-colored, scooped, striped, louvered, spoiler-clad monsters launched themselves out of the lights with a variety of engines, including a Hemi, 440 Six Pack, Cobra Jet, W-30, Stage 1, RA IV, and an LS6 454. Despite pinnacle offerings (or more accurately, because of them), the 1970 muscle-car sales suffered backlash. This smorgasbord of excess invoked penalizing big-block insurance rates.

Although John DeLorean had departed Pontiac to helm Chevrolet, the residue of his disdain for budget Pontiacs marked the 1970-model-year lineup at their introduction on September 18, 1969. Dealers noted that small-block Trans-Am-race-series homologation cars had big-block-style looks. What if the same thing was attempted with a cheaper small-block? The lower-horsepower small-blocks had more low-end torque. Dealers recognized the appeal of a "Junior GTO Judge" from the perspective of the initial cost, operating expenses, and insurance premiums. Several dealerships took action.

Jury by Carter and Stampede

Carter Pontiac Buick in Burnaby, British Columbia, Canada, and Stampede Pontiac Buick Ltd. in Calgary, Alberta, Canada, created a specialty LeMans named "the Jury." It was marketed in conjunction with the GTO Judge option, which was expensive and elusive in Canada. Even if you had the money, dealer allotments of Judges were sparse in Canada. The Jury paired the Judge's appearance with inventory volume.

Carter and Stampede special-ordered 50 Palladium Silver LeMans two-door pillar coupes with blue bench seats and a 350 2-barrel, 255-hp engine. The special order included a 3.90:1 axle, which was normally only obtainable in a Ram Air IV GTO. The run of 50 LeMans were built during the fourth week of October 1969 with a mix of automatic and manual-shift cars.

A single offset stripe ran the length of the hood and decklid on the Jury. (Photo Courtesy Duncan Brown)

A 50-Car Order

It is believed that General Motors required a minimum of 50 duplicate cars ordered when non-production options were requested. The 3.90:1 axle in the Carter/Stampede LeMans order was not available with the 350 engine, which defaulted to a 2.56:1 for cars with an automatic transmission or 3.23:1 for manual transmissions.

Dealership Jury Modifications

Carter and Stampede added graphics and hood pins. Both dealers added a rally stripe down the hood on the driver's side as well as a similar stripe wrapped around the rear quarters and over the rear decklid.

Carter placed the unique fireball Jury logo just aft of the front fenders. Stampede placed it over the rear quarter-panel stripe. Carter mounted a pedestal-style black 1970 Judge spoiler to the rear decklid. Stampede added a body-color 1969-style Judge spoiler to the rear decklid.

The 3.90:1 axle substantially boosted the 350's acceleration. The Jury was a total package with power front disc brakes, Rally II Pontiac

I imagine the conversation went something like this. "Well, how are we going to put a callout on the silver and black LeMans that people can see?" "Let's make it as bright as the sun!"

Well, at least it has flames. (Photo Courtesy Duncan Brown)

Motor Division (PMD) mag wheels, GR70-14 BFGoodrich radial tires, and medium-stiff suspension.

Jury Verdict

A Jury 4-speed cost $4,346.00 at Carter and $4,236.50 at Stampede. The Jury 350 engine triggered insurance savings compared to big-block rates. The Jury gas and insurance savings could be added back into the car as performance upgrades.

Compared to the original Pontiac E/T concept, the Jury was just as wild looking, but the 350 was milder than the E/T's 350 H.O. The Jury 2-barrel carburetor, moderate heads, and single exhaust provided decent stoplight launches with the 3.90:1 axle. The axle made the package lively enough for many as it stood and wouldn't embarrass the hot shot in the interim before an upgrade to a 4-barrel carburetor, headers, and dual exhaust.

Knafel Magnum 400

Two months after the Jury debut, Knafel Pontiac in Akron, Ohio, announced a run of 50 budget GTOs named the "Magnum 400" on December 18, 1969. Magnums cost a mere $2,995.00. Knafel added a big-valve GTO 400 engine, an M21 4-speed transmission, a 3.90:1 axle, and heavy-duty suspension to a stripped, bench-seat 1970 Tempest pillar coupe. Knafel added 1969 Judge stripes and a name sticker reminiscent of the Judge's psychedelic identifier. None of the Magnum 400s survived the Ohio winter road salt.

Jury Spurs E/T Rebirth

By the mid-1970 model year, factories took a stab at high-visibility junior super-car packages. Hurst/Olds created a dynamite-looking

Stampede Pontiac Buick Ltd. spread the word locally regarding its performance vehicles. I imagine that naming a car the Executioner would have been taking things too far. (Photo Courtesy Duncan Brown)

package for a small-block screamer that Oldsmobile eventually built in-house as the Rallye 350 and released it on February 18, 1970.

The hierarchal positioning of Pontiac above Chevrolet dispersed as DeLorean's departure set in. Pontiac stooped down into a bargain intermediate Pontiac named the "T-37" ("T" for Tempest, and "37" is Pontiac's internal code for a two-door hardtop). The T-37 was a gutted stripper that was priced cheaper than a Chevelle. Longtime Pontiac ad man Jim Wangers was mortified by the degradation implicit in undoing the brand's established market position.

Degradation aside, the T-37 was an ideal starting point for a budget muscle machine. On May 15, 1970, Pontiac debuted a junior muscle car named the GT-37, which was based on the T-37 platform. Like the Jury and Magnum, it had a spartan interior. Like the Jury, it came with hood pins, stripes, and Rally II PMD mags. Like the Jury, it had the 350 2-barrel carburetor standard. The GT-37 edged the Jury and equaled the Magnum 400 with dual exhaust and splitters, plus heavy-duty suspension.

Although the GT-37 had a Hurst floor shifter, it was a 3-speed. Both the Jury and Magnum 400 provided four speeds when manual shift was chosen. The GT-37 could be ordered with a 400, and if it was teamed to a 4-speed, the factory installed the GTO engine by default. This move was likely inspired by the Magnum 400 setup.

Jury Legacy

The Jury wasn't the fastest dealer-special small-block of 1970. Don Yenko's Nova Deuce was probably the sneakiest and most savage of the 1970 juniors. The 350 engine that sounded harmless on the insurance agent's paperwork was a screaming solid-lifter LT-1. The Jury wasn't the craziest-looking small-block. That distinction is held by the Oldsmobile Rallye 350.

However, the Jury was one of the earliest juniors and inspired some factory trends. The Jury anticipated the coming wave of great-looking insurable 2-barrel small-blocks. Prior junior muscle was usually a 4-barrel, dual-exhaust motor mated to heads from a bigger engine.

In 1971, the Maverick Grabber became its own series with the 302 2-barrel. The 1971 Duster Twister had wild proprietary graphics but a 318 2-barrel ceiling for the engines. The Heavy Chevy appeared in the mid-1971 model year and copied the GT-37 that continued its 1970 concept.

The year after the Jury special-ordered 3.90:1 axles were available, General Motors raised axle ratios across the board to compensate for lower-compression 1971-model-year engines.

1 of 1 Jury

John Beal bought his Jury off the Stampede lot on September 4, 1970. Within one week, John switched out the intake and carburetor for a 4-barrel Holley. The progressive equipment upgrade was typical of many Jury or GT-37 owners. Later, as his time and budget allowed, John added headers and dual exhaust with splitters. John replaced the blue two-spoke steering wheel with a Grant wood-rim steering wheel and placed an aftermarket tachometer in the empty clock pod. Under-dash gauges and an aftermarket stereo soon followed.

The Jury was passed to John's son Grai, who retained the Day 2 modifications made by his father. Currently, a collector owns this 1 of 1 cutting-edge trendsetter.

1973 NICKEY CHEVROLET NOVA

By Wes Eisenschenk

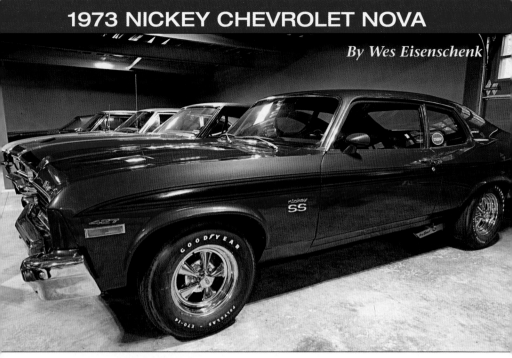

Like the rug that ties the room together, this paint color goes well with the Nickey and 427 emblems, traction bars, Cragar wheels, and Nickey decal on this 1973 SS Nova. (Photo Courtesy Wenona Suydam)

Nickey Chevrolet, which is famously recognized by the backward letter "k" in its name, was located at 4501 W. Irving Park Rd. in Chicago, Illinois. The dealership is often cited as one of the key tuner/builders of performance-oriented Chevrolets during the muscle-car era.

The dealership dates back to the mid-1920s, but it was brothers Ed and Jack Stephani who took the reins of Nickey in the late 1950s and turned the face of the company (and a letter) around from a mundane dealership into one with country-wide recognition. In fact, it was Jack, while on vacation in Florida, who came up with using a backward letter as a marketing component to change the perception of Nickey Chevrolet.

The implemented reversed "k" in Nickey in its signage was often reported as incorrect to the staff at the dealership. With no good deed going unpunished, Nickey offered a voucher for an upside-down cake (pun intended) at a local bakery for those who offered the helpful advice. I imagine that perusing the showroom floor was gifted to the considerate soul as well.

Road Racing

Ed and Jack dove into selling performance automobiles by going road racing in 1958, first with a Scarab and then a series of Corvettes. They raced under the nickname "Purple People Eater" on their, you guessed it, purple race cars.

With hard-charging Jim Jeffords behind the wheel, Nickey Chevrolet won B Production Championships in 1958 and 1959 and won 27 out of 30 SCCA races. It was reported in 1959 that the Scarab cost $75,000 to build.

Nickey continued with road-racing sponsorship throughout the early 1960s in SCCA and United States Road Racing Championship (USRRC) competition and expanded its sponsorship in the Mobil Economy Run that ran from Los Angeles to New York.

Drag Racing

As much success as Nickey Chevrolet had with road-racing cars, the next natural step was to transition into drag racing as the booming muscle-car market took shape. Nickey brought "Mr. Chevrolet" Dick Harrell on board as its performance advisor at the dealership and partnered with him to sponsor his 1966 Chevy II Nova on the drag strip. It was this partnership with Harrell that is often described as the beginning of the super-car conversion era for Chevrolet muscle cars.

If you were expecting bucket seats, three pedals, and a roll bar, think again. A Sun Super Tack and a 103-octane label provided everything that was necessary to vanquish the car in the other lane. (Photo Courtesy Wenona Suydam)

With Harrell giving Nickey drag-racing credibility, the next logical step was to brand Nickey Chevrolet as the go-to place for Chevrolet muscle cars. In a letter that was sent to Nickey Chevrolet and addressed to Dick Harrell, the American Hot Rod Association (AHRA), noted the following: "This is to advise you that our technical committee has certified the legality of the following engines for the 1967 Camaro. This will be a dealer option, and until further notice, work must be performed by Nickey Chevrolet or its agent. The engines are the 427 Chev, 396 Chev, and a high-performance 352-inch engine. These cars will be eligible for regular formula class participation during the 1967 AHRA drag racing season."

With that, Nickey was in the world of super-car conversion.

Nickey Street Cars

With Mr. Chevrolet filling orders at Nickey Chevrolet, the first conversions took place in October 1966. The Camaro was Nickey's conversion of choice for 1967. No official numbers exist on how many Camaros were converted, but evidence from old classified ads suggest a healthy number. Harrell campaigned a 1967 Camaro for Nickey for part of the year and ultimately began the first Camaro super-car conversions for Don Yenko as well.

The year 1968 saw a continuation of Camaro super-car conversions. The following year brought about the COPO 427 Camaro and Chevelle and threw a wrench into Nickey's Camaro super-car conversion plans. The alternative was the Chevrolet Nova.

Even the central office production order (COPO) program wasn't absent-minded enough to have 427 Novas fleet ordered. This gap in the ordering system created an opportunity for Nickey Chevrolet to convert Novas into some incredibly wicked machines.

With Chevrolet offering 427 cars in 1969 and lifting its over-400-ci-displacement ban for 1970 (454 Chevelles and El Caminos), Nickey concentrated on building existing performance cars for customers until 1973.

1973 427 Novas

Nickey couldn't leave well enough alone. In the May 1973 issue of *Hot Rod* magazine, Nickey sent a 1973 L88 Nova to California for Performance Editor C.J. Baker to photograph and feature for the cover

Wayne McDonald received refunds on his Illinois sales tax and airfare after flying to New York to pick up his 1973 Nickey Nova. (Photo Courtesy Kevin Suydam)

Big-block engines weren't strangers to Nova subframes, but the factory hadn't used one between the Nova's fenders since 1970. By 1973, Nickey Chevrolet was the last one that pumped the large engines into Novas. (Photo Courtesy Wenona Suydam)

story. When all was said and done, the Nova was rung out to the tune of 12.03 at 116.57 mph. Just like that, Nickey Chevrolet was thrust right back into the super-car market as the muscle-car market was coming to an end.

Wayne McDonald of Prospect, New York, was one of the people mesmerized by a new car that ran that fast in 1973. Wayne chose a Dark Red car from Nickey's inventory for conversion and flew to Chicago to pick up his purpose-built hot rod after he paid the lofty sum of $4,200.

It didn't take Wayne long to figure out that everything wasn't as it seemed with the Nova. For starters, the stock front springs were still in the car and made drivability a bit of a challenge. Out back, there was a 2.71 rear end that struggled to get the car from stoplight to stoplight. The Nova's original 3/8-inch fuel line and big 850-cfm Holley carburetor seemed to disagree with each other, and a bashed-in header pipe made breathability a bit on the rough side. Inside, 3/8-inch pushrods for rocker arms with 7/16-inch guide plates required the heads to be pulled and the valves replaced from the wrong-sized guides.

After quite a bit of sorting out, Wayne got the car running well and even claimed to make a flying 160-mph pass for a prospective buyer years later. Wayne owned the car until March 1979, and finally relinquished the car to someone local. As time passed, Wayne remembered the Nova as just another former car.

The Rise of Super-Car Collecting

As the 1970s turned into the 1980s, and then into the 1990s, nostalgia for these old dealer-built super cars began to rise. Enthusiasts and collectors sought out the odd and rare, and Don Yenko's cars led the charge into the current era of collecting. As more cars were featured in muscle-car magazines and on TV shows, collectors began to assemble pedigree collections of these super cars.

Kevin Suydam of Washington has one of these impressive collections. His website, corvettes-musclecars.com, features the most original, pristine, and influential cars of the entire muscle-car era. Chevrolet super cars from Dana Chevrolet, Baldwin-Motion, Yenko, Berger Chevrolet, Dick Harrell, and Nickey Chevrolet are all on display in his collection. The newest car in his collection happens to be Wayne McDonald's 1973 Nickey L88 427 Nova.

1973 YENKO 427 CAMARO

By Tom Clary

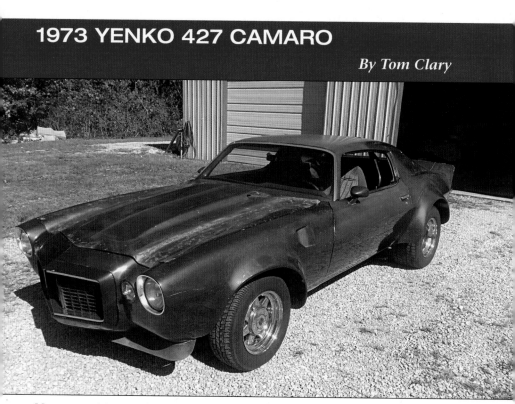

Many consider 1971 to be the last year for Yenko Super Cars—sans the 1981 Turbo Z, with the Yenko Vega Stinger. However, Don had one more trick up his sleeve. This 1973 Yenko Camaro was ordered new through Yenko dealer Jay Kline Chevrolet. (Photo Courtesy Tom Clary)

This is the car that Don Yenko and Yenko Chevrolet "never built." Sometimes there are rumors of cars that are too rare and unique for one to believe that they exist. This story is about one of those rumors, which turned out to be fact and not fiction.

For the past 25-plus years, Yenko enthusiasts have debated whether Yenko Chevrolet ever built a second-generation Camaro besides the 1981 Turbo Z. It was not only debated whether Yenko ever built any Camaros in the early 1970s, but if Yenko did, was it powered by a big-block or small-block?

One More Super Car

In the early 1970s, numerous magazine articles, advertisements, and stories alluded to such, but there were no known documented examples. Little did they know that a 1973 Yenko Camaro was quietly resting in the original owner's garage near Minneapolis, Minnesota.

By chance, in early 2000, Tom Clary, a Yenko collector and founder of the Yenko Sportscar Club, happened to stumble upon information related to the elusive Camaro. After a few days of research, Tom tracked down the car and its owner. Although it was not for sale at the time, Tom contacted the owner every few years to check on the status of the car.

Finally, in late 2020, the car was finally for sale, and a deal was made. Tom and his family would become caretakers of the rare Camaro. Shortly thereafter, Tom and his wife made the trek to Minnesota to pick up the car. While they were there, they spent time with the original owner and his wife as he reminisced about the adventures of owning such a rare car.

Jay Kline Chevrolet: Yenko Dealer

The car, serial number YSC 730001, was purchased from Jay Kline Chevrolet Company in Minneapolis, Minnesota, on August 9, 1973, as a new car, complete with the warranty book, owner's manual, and Yenko tech manual. The original invoice from Jay Kline showed that the Yenko 427 conversion cost $2,500 with a total price of $7,832.32, which was a hefty sum for an automobile in 1973.

The Build

Yenko Chevrolet started with a new 1973 Camaro coupe that was Dark Green with a green interior and had LT/RS options with the Z/28 package. Yenko made numerous modifications to the drivetrain and appearance. The small-block Chevy 350 was replaced with a 427-ci, 450-hp aluminum-headed solid-lifter engine. Other modifications included a steel hood with a fiberglass raised cowl-induction section, an air cleaner with a special hood seal that was coupled with ram-air ducts in openings behind the grille, and a Yenko-modified Super GT Hydro 400 heavy-duty transmission with a remote cooler. Also installed was a Yenko-modified Chevrolet heavy-duty 12-bolt Positraction rear end with 3:73 gears in place of the stock 10-bolt rear end, a one-piece steel front-end with Trans Am–type air extractors, front and rear spoilers, front and rear fender flares, an extended trunk

Unrestored and in original condition, this 1973 Yenko Camaro is the last confirmed big-block transplant car converted by Don Yenko. (Photo Courtesy Tom Clary)

and modified rear jump seat, a 150-mph speedometer, an in-dash cable-driven tachometer, slotted mag wheels with BFGoodrich radial tires and 427 emblems, and a trunk-mounted battery.

Special Yenko badging/decals included gold-tone Yenko emblems on the tail panel, glove box, and tachometer, and a metal Don Yenko identification plate on the driver-side front-pillar post. On the core support is an emissions 427 engine decal, aluminum head warning decal, and "Off-Road Use Only" sticker. The air cleaner lid has a "Don Yenko Sportscars" decal. On the end of the door, decals state that this prototype does not meet federal emissions or safety standards. There are also special jacking instructions under the trunk lid because of the modified front end.

Well Documented

This Camaro could be the most documented Yenko ever sold. It has the original title, security agreement, and note from the lending institution as well as the original invoice from Jay Kline Chevrolet with receipts. There is paperwork stamped with "Yenko Sportscars Drawer 520, Canonsburg, Pennsylvania," that includes the 1973 Chevrolet Camaro owner's manual, 1973 Chevrolet new vehicle warranty book with an embossed Protect-O-Plate, 1973 Chevrolet consumer information booklet, and a letter from Yenko Sportscars, Inc. The letter featured special instructions that outline how to install a front license plate on the one-piece front end. Specially prepared by Yenko, a 20-page owner's manual details the build, makeup, and other special features of the car that often mentions why Don used certain parts, such as installing a 427-ci engine versus the more readily available 454-ci engine.

According to the manual, the prototype ran the quarter mile in the low-13-second range. It stated that this was with a steel front end. With lighter fiberglass front-end components, the car should run mid-12s, and low 11s in race trim.

This Car's to be Seen!

The car is unrestored and is in good condition overall. The paint and small portions of sheet metal show the years of being a daily driver and the effects of sitting out in Minnesota weather. When purchased from the original owner, it was noted that the original engine was long gone—it was replaced by a small-block Chevrolet engine. It also had late-model aftermarket wheels, and a few other odds and ends. While maintaining the car's unrestored condition, thanks to vintage pictures and the Yenko tech manual, every attempt was made to put the car back the way it was originally built, complete with a 427-ci aluminum-headed engine, correct exhaust, and slotted mags with BFGoodrich tires.

When the car is shown, the first question usually is, "Is it a real Yenko?"

The second question usually is, "Are you going to restore it?" Although the car is far from perfect, a car is only original once. Because the car is so unique with so many modifications, there are no plans to restore the car.

The third question is, "What is it worth?" That's anyone's guess, as there's really nothing to compare it to since it is a 1 of 1, prototype, the last 427 Yenko Camaro built, the only second-generation 427 Yenko Camaro built, has more modifications than any known

Yenko, and the list of one-offs goes on and on. Until it is listed for sale, no one really knows.

Although such rare cars are often tucked away in a museum or private collection and rarely seen by the public, anyone who knows the Clary family will tell you that they do not allow their cars to gather dust in their shop. The 1973 Yenko Camaro is a Sunday driver that attends local cruise-ins, shows, and maybe even the local drag strip.

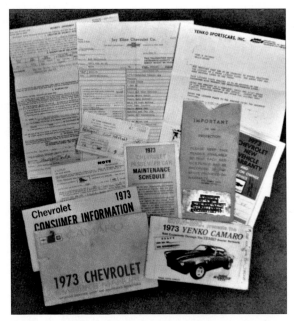

An impressive pile of documentation authenticates the validity of the 1973 Yenko Camaro. (Photo Courtesy Tom Clary)

Additional books that may interest you...

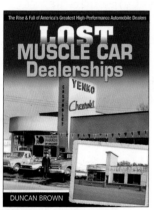

LOST MUSCLE CAR DEALERSHIPS
by Duncan Brown
Revisit the glorious 1960s and early 1970s, when cars from Reynolds Buick, Yeakel Chrysler-Plymouth, Mel Burns Ford, and others created the lasting muscle car legacy through innovative advertising and over-the-top performance. Detailed text and more than 250 historic photos and illustrations provide the history of those dealerships. 8.5 x 11", 192 pgs, 360 photos, Sftbd. ISBN 9781613254516 Part # CT644

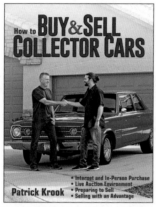

HOW TO BUY AND SELL COLLECTOR CARS
by Patrick Krook
As the owner of REV! Muscle Cars, author Patrick Krook has located, bought, and sold hundreds of investment-quality cars for collectors. This book takes you from being a novice to a seasoned buyer/seller while enjoying the adventure. 8.5 x 11", 160 pgs, 247 photos, Sftbd. ISBN 9781613255469 Part # CT668

MUSCLE CAR SPECIAL EDITIONS
by Duncan Brown
Special-edition muscle cars are the highest valued and most collectible cars from American automotive manufacturers that were produced between 1961 and 1974. Muscle car historian Duncan Brown takes us through these special-edition muscle cars, their creators, and the behind-the-scenes forces that shaped these wild beasts into legends that left a lasting legacy. 8.5 x 11", 192 pgs, 390 photos, Hdbd. ISBN 9781613255797 Part # CT673

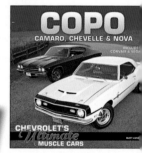

COPO CAMARO, CHEVELLE & NOVA: Chevrolet's Ultimate Muscle Cars
by Matt Avery
Chevy muscle car aficionado and author Matt Avery retraces the history of the COPO program and the creation of these premium muscle cars. He has scoured archives and tracked down owners and personnel involved in the program to deliver a comprehensive story and complete guide to COPO cars. 10 x 10", 204 pgs, 400 photos, Hdbd. ISBN 9781613253915 Part # CT6...